— The Unofficial Guide to
Walt Disney World® —

D1212087

The Unofficial Guide to
Walt Disney World®

Bob Sehlinger
John Finley

Menasha Ridge Press

Distributed exclusively by
Simon & Schuster, New York, New York

Copyright © 1985 by Robert W. Sehlinger
and John Finley

All rights reserved including the right of
reproduction in whole or in part in any form

Published by Menasha Ridge Press
by arrangement with
Simon & Schuster, Inc.
  Simon & Schuster Building
  Rockefeller Center
  1230 Avenue of the Americas
  New York, New York 10020

Manufactured in the United States of America

Library of Congress Cataloging in Publication Data
Sehlinger, Bob, 1945–
    The unofficial guide to Walt Disney World.

    Includes index.
    1. Walt Disney World (Fla.)—Guide-books.
I. Finley, John, 1938–   . II. Title.
GV1853.3.F620747 1985   791'.06'875924   85-21375
ISBN: 0-671-60494-5 (Simon & Schuster : pbk.)

10 9 8 7 6 5 4 3 2 1

ISBN: 0-671-60494-5

Declaration of Independence

The authors and researchers of this guide specifically and categorically declare that they are and always have been totally independent of Walt Disney Productions, Inc., of Disneyland, Inc., of Walt Disney World, Inc., and of any and all other members of the Disney corporate family not listed.

The material in this guide originated with the authors and researchers and has not been reviewed, edited, or in any way approved by Walt Disney Productions, Inc., Disneyland, Inc., or Walt Disney World, Inc.

Trademarks

The following attractions, shows, components, entities, etc., mentioned or discussed in this guide are registered trademarks of Walt Disney Productions, Inc.:

> Adventureland
> AudioAnimatronics
> Disneyland
> EPCOT
> Fantasyland
> Magic Kingdom
> New Orleans Square
> PeopleMover
> Space Mountain
> Walt Disney
> Walt Disney World

New trademarks are applied for almost continuously. These will be recognized as and when appropriate in subsequent editions of this guide.

Contents

—— *Acknowledgments* ——

Special thanks to our field research team who rendered a Herculean effort in what must have seemed like a fantasy version of Sartre's *No Exit* to the tune of *It's a Small World*. We hope you all recover to tour another day.

Ray Westbrook
Joan W. Burns
Cyril C. Sehlinger
Pid Rafter
Karin Zachow
Paul Owens
Mary Mitchell

Many thanks also to Barbara Williams and Teresa Smith for the design and production of this book. Tseng Information Systems earned our sincere appreciation by keeping tight deadlines in providing the typography.

— The Unofficial Guide to
Walt Disney World —

How Come "Unofficial"?

This Guidebook represents the first comprehensive *critical* appraisal of Walt Disney World. Its purpose is to provide the reader with the information necessary to tour the Magic Kingdom and EPCOT Center with the greatest efficiency and economy, and with the least amount of hassle and standing in line. The authors of this guide believe in the wondrous variety, joy, and excitement of the Disney attractions. At the same time, we recognize realistically that Walt Disney World is a business, with the same profit motivations as businesses the world over.

Just as it is impossible for an attorney to represent both sides in the same case, so, too, we believe it is impossible for an "official guide" to serve both Walt Disney World and the consumer. Walt Disney World naturally wants you to stay in its hotels, to eat in its restaurants, and tour its attractions. An "official guide" should be a sourcebook of information designed to enhance the appeal of the Disney offering. Tips that would shorten your visit or criticisms, no matter how well founded, that guide you away from Disney eateries, lodging, and shops would have no place in an "official guide."

In this guide we have elected to represent and serve you, the consumer. Its contents were researched and compiled by a team of evaluators who were, and are, completely independent of Walt Disney World and its parent corporation. If a restaurant serves bad food, or a gift item is overpriced, or a certain ride isn't worth the wait, we can say so, and in the process, hopefully make your visit more fun, efficient, and economical.

How This Guide Was Researched and Written

While much has been written concerning Walt Disney World, very little has been comparative or evaluative. Most guides simply parrot Disney World's own promotional material. In preparing this guide, however, nothing was taken for granted. Each theme park was visited at different times throughout the year by a team of trained observers. They conducted detailed evaluations and rated each theme park with all its component rides, shows, exhibits, services, and concessions according to a formal, pretested rating instrument. Interviews with attraction patrons were conducted to determine what tourists—of all age groups—enjoyed most and least during their Disney World visit.

While our observers were independent and impartial, we do not claim special expertise or scientific background relative to the types of exhibits, performances, or attractions. Like you, we visit Walt Disney World as tourists, noting our satisfaction or dissatisfaction. We do not believe it necessary then to be an agronomist to know whether we enjoyed the agricultural exhibits in the EPCOT Center Land pavilion. Disney offerings are marketed to the touring public, and it is as the public that we have experienced them.

The primary difference between the average tourist and the trained evaluator is in the evaluator's professional skills in organization, preparation, and observation. The trained evaluator is responsible for much more than simply observing and cataloging. While the tourist seated next to him is being entertained and delighted by the Tropical Serenade (Enchanted Tiki Birds) in the Magic Kingdom, the professional is rating the performance in terms of theme, pace, continuity, and originality. He or she is also checking out the physical arrangements: Is the sound system clear and audible without being overpowering; is the audience shielded from the sun or from the rain; is seating adequate; can everyone in the audience clearly see the staging area? And what about guides and/or performers: Are they knowledgeable, articulate, and professional in their presentation; are they friendly and engaging? Does the performance begin and end on time; does the show contain the features described in Disney World's promotional literature? These and many other considerations figure prominently in the rating of any staged performance. Similarly, detailed and relevant checklists were prepared and applied by observer teams to rides, exhibits, concessions, and to the theme parks in general. Finally observations and evaluator ratings were integrated with audience reactions and the opinions of patrons to compile a comprehensive quality profile of each feature and service.

In compiling this guide, we recognize the fact that a tourist's age, sex, background, and interests will strongly influence his or her taste in Walt Disney World offerings and will account for a preference of one ride or feature over another. Given this fact we make no attempt at comparing apples with oranges. How indeed could a meaningful comparison be made between the priceless historic artifacts in the Mexican pavilion of EPCOT Center and the wild roller coaster ride of the Magic Kingdom's Space Mountain? Instead, our objective is to provide the reader with sufficient description, critical evaluation, and pertinent data to make knowledgeable decisions according to individual tastes.

The essence of this guide, therefore, consists of individual critiques and descriptions of each feature of the Magic Kingdom and EPCOT Center, and several detailed Touring Plans to help you avoid bottlenecks and crowds.

Walt Disney World—An Overview

If you are selecting among the tourist attractions in Florida, the question is not whether to visit Walt Disney World but how to see the best of the various Disney offerings with some economy of time, effort, and finances.

Make no mistake, there is nothing on earth quite like Walt Disney World. Incredible in its scope, genius, beauty, and imagination, it is a joy and wonder for people of all ages. A fantasy, a dream, and a vision all rolled into one, it transcends simple entertainment, making us children and adventurers, freeing us for an hour or a day to live the dreams of our past, present, and future.

Certainly we are critics, but it is the responsibility of critics to credit that which is done well as surely as to reflect negatively on that which is done poorly. The Disney attractions are special, a quantum leap beyond and above any man-made entertainment offering we know of. We cannot understand how anyone could visit Florida and bypass Walt Disney World.

What Walt Disney World Encompasses

Walt Disney World encompasses forty-three square miles, an area twice the size of Manhattan Island. Situated strategically in this vast expanse are two major theme parks, two minor theme parks, a major hotel/eating/shopping complex, several golf courses, an enormous campground, four large interconnected lakes, a permanent nature preserve, and a complete internal transportation system consisting of four-lane highways, an elevated monorail, and a system of canals.

Most tourists refer to the entire Florida Disney facility as Walt Disney World, or more simply, as Disney World. The Magic Kingdom and EPCOT Center are thought of as being "in" Disney World. Other visitors refer to the Magic Kingdom as Disney World and EPCOT Center as EPCOT, and are not sure exactly how to label the entity as a whole. The Disney spokesmen, alas, are of no help to anyone.

Totally ignoring popular usage, they insist on calling the overall facility EPCOT, not to be confused with the theme park which they label EPCOT Center. Thus, in official parlance, EPCOT Center is in EPCOT. Also in EPCOT is the Vacation Kingdom which consists of the Magic Kingdom and the Theme Resorts (Contemporary Resort Hotel, Polynesian Village, Golf Resort, and Fort Wilderness Campground). In our description we will refer to the total Disney facility as Walt Disney World according to popular tradition, and will consider the Magic Kingdom, EPCOT Center, and everything else that sits on that forty-three-square-mile chunk of real estate to be included in the overall designation. Whew!

— The Major Theme Parks —

The Magic Kingdom

The Magic Kingdom is what most people think of when they think of Walt Disney World. It is the collection of adventures, rides, and shows symbolized by the Disney cartoon characters and Cinderella Castle. Although the Magic Kingdom is only one element of the Disney attraction complex, it remains the heart of Disney World. The Magic Kingdom is divided into six subareas or "lands" arranged around a central hub. First encountered is Main Street, U.S.A., which connects the Magic Kingdom entrance with the central hub. Moving clockwise around the hub, the other lands are Adventureland, Frontierland, Liberty Square, Fantasyland, and Tomorrowland. Main Street and the other five lands will be described in detail later. Two hotel complexes, the Contemporary Resort Hotel and the Polynesian Village, are located close to the Magic Kingdom and are directly connected to it by monorail and by boat.

EPCOT Center

EPCOT (Experimental Prototype Community of Tomorrow) Center is the newer of the major Disney Florida theme parks, having opened in October of 1982. Divided into two major areas, Future World and World Showcase, the park is twice the size of and is comparable in scope to the Magic Kingdom. Future World consists of a number of futuristic pavilions, each relating to a different theme concerning man's creativity and technological advancement. World Showcase, arranged around a forty-one-acre lagoon, presents the architectural, social, and cultural heritages of almost a dozen nations, with each country represented by famous landmarks and local settings familiar to world travelers. EPCOT Center is generally more educationally oriented than the Magic Kingdom and has been repeatedly characterized as a sort of permanent world's fair. Unlike the Magic Kingdom, which Disney spokesmen represent as being essentially complete, EPCOT Center is pictured as a continually changing and growing entity. At present there are no lodging accommodations situated on or close to EPCOT Center (the closest being the Contemporary Resort Hotel and the Polynesian Village). EPCOT Center is connected to the Magic Kingdom and resort hotels by monorail.

— *The Minor Theme Parks* —

Discovery Island

Situated in Bay Lake close to the Magic Kingdom, Discovery Island is a tropically landscaped, small zoological park primarily featuring birdlife. Small intimate trails wind through the exotic foliage, contrasting with the broad thoroughfares of the major theme parks. The island is small and takes an hour or two to see in its entirety. There are no lodging accommodations. Access is exclusively by boat from the main Bay Lake docks (Magic Kingdom Dock, Fort Wilderness Landing, Resort Hotels' docks).

River Country

Also located on Bay Lake, River Country is within the Fort Wilderness Campground. A swimming and sunning theme park, River Country features a heated pool, a beach on Bay Lake, water slides, and a whitewater innertube ride among other things. There are no lodging accommodations. Access is by bus from the Transportation and Ticket Center (junction and transfer point for EPCOT Center and Magic Kingdom monorails) or from the River Country parking lot on Vista Boulevard (see map, page 23).

— *Other Walt Disney World Development Areas* —

Walt Disney World Village

A large shopping/eating/lodging complex. Walt Disney World Village lodging accommodations are second only to the Contemporary and Polynesian Resorts in terms of proximity to the major theme parks (geographically they are actually closer to EPCOT Center than the two resorts). The Walt Disney World Villas, part of the Village complex, are the only lodging accommodations in Walt Disney World proper which offer kitchen facilities. A small grocery is conveniently located in the shopping complex. Other Village facilities include tennis, golf, and a conference center. Access to other parts of Walt Disney World from Walt Disney World Village is by shuttle bus or private automobile.

Fort Wilderness Campground

A spacious resort campground for both tent and RV camping. Air-conditioned trailers are available for rent. Features of the Fort Wilderness Campground include full RV hookups, evening entertainment, a group camping area, horseback riding, bike trails, jogging trails, and a petting farm. River Country is situated in the Fort Wilderness Campground. Access to the Magic Kingdom and Discovery Island is via boat from the Fort Wilderness Landing, or to the Magic Kingdom and EPCOT Center via shuttle bus or private automobile.

Golf Resort Hotel

Located on Asian Way at the western end of Seven Seas Lagoon, the Golf Resort offers lodging, dining, and 72 holes of golf. Access to other areas of Walt Disney World is via shuttle bus or private automobile.

PART ONE—Planning

Before You Leave Home

Gathering Information

In addition to this guide, information concerning Walt Disney World can be obtained at the public library, through travel agencies, or by writing or calling:

Walt Disney World Company
Department GL, Box 40
Lake Buena Vista, FL 32830
Phone (305) 824-4321

Many books are available through retail booksellers which deal in whole or in part with Walt Disney World. Unfortunately, many are pre-EPCOT Center and therefore obsolete, or alternatively regurgitate Disney promotional literature or only provide a superficial overview. A comprehensive sourcebook is the Disney publication *Walt Disney World* by Stephen Birnbaum, published by Houghton Mifflin Company and Diversion Communications, Inc.

Since this is the "Official Guide" to Walt Disney World (WDW), you can expect lots of current information but not much in the way of criticism. The Birnbaum guide is very strong on background (how tall Big Thunder Mountain is and how long it took to build, etc.), but very weak on practical touring information, i.e., how to avoid the crowds.

While our guide deals very specifically with hassle-free touring of the major theme parks, the "Official Guide" provides immense detail concerning lodging and restaurants, both in and outside of Walt Disney World. The Birnbaum guide is also the best sourcebook for non-theme-park offerings at Walt Disney World (swimming, boating, golf, tennis, fishing, shopping, etc.).

Timing Your Visit

—— *Trying to Reason with the Tourist Season* ——

It is one of the objectives of this book to assist the tourist, when possible, in avoiding crowds. It is useful therefore to understand the overall seasonality and traffic flow of Florida tourism.

Peninsular Florida (all of Florida except the Panhandle) has two peak seasons. One begins just before Christmas and ends just after Easter and is referred to as the "Winter Season" or sometimes just "the Season." The other, known as the "Summer Season" or "Family Season," gets into swing about the middle of June and lasts until late August.

Christmas Week, which effectively kicks off the Winter Season, is Florida's busiest week of the year, with facilities throughout the state (including attractions), being pushed to their limit. Many attractions offer special programs beginning several days prior to Christmas and extending through New Year's Day. Crowds, however, are awesome, with many smaller attractions inundated and long waits in line the norm at larger attractions. Because of the crowded conditions, we do not recommend Christmas Week for attraction touring. If, however, your schedule permits arriving the preceding week (say December 15th or thereabouts) crowds are manageable and sometimes even sparse. Get your touring in by the 22nd and then relax and enjoy the beach over Christmas.

Though the mammoth throngs of Christmas Week dissipate following New Year's Day, the Winter Season remains in full session with heavy attraction attendance through Easter. Easter Week is almost as congested as Christmas Week. During the Winter Season a high concentration of tourists are a fact of life.

The period between Easter and the beginning of the Summer Season in early June is usually slow and is a particularly good time for attraction touring. Activity picks up again toward the middle of June with the arrival of the family vacation traffic. This second season runs through late August when the kids return to school.

Attendance at individual attractions varies, with some attractions more popular with the Winter Season tourist and others more popular with the Summer Season tourist. This is attributable in part to the relatively small number of school-age children present during Winter Season.

September through mid-December is very slow throughout Florida except for the Thanksgiving holiday period. Our research team felt that the nicest time to visit Florida in terms of weather, low-stress touring, and crowd avoidance was the first two weeks in December, just prior to the Christmas crunch.

Holiday weekends throughout the year, as well as special events (Florida Derby, space craft launchings, auto races, local festivals, etc.) precipitate heavy attraction attendance in and out of season. On days immediately preceding or following the holiday periods, however, attendance is often extremely light.

The best weather in Florida usually occurs between late fall and mid-April, which coincides, of course, with the busy Winter Season. Attraction touring is pleasant throughout the day, though mornings and late afternoons are best for crowd avoidance during this time of the year.

During the warmer months of the Summer Season, comfort as well as crowd avoidance suggest early day touring.

Rainy days in both the Summer and Winter Seasons often afford excellent opportunities for beating the crowd. Many outdoor attractions offer good protection from the elements and are as enjoyable on a rainy day as on a sunny day. Indoor attractions see their heaviest attendance on rainy days. Here we recommend touring on sunny days during the very hot midday hours (11:30 A.M.–2:30 P.M.).

Off season (mid-April through early June and September through mid-December) touring is characterized by smaller crowds and by somewhat rainier weather, and is generally an excellent time to visit the state's premier, large scale attractions. However, since attendance is lightest at these times it is not uncommon for certain major rides, shows, and exhibits to be closed for maintenance or revision. A phone call to the attraction under consideration will obtain information concerning which, if any, key features will be out of action during your intended visit.

The Florida Panhandle has a somewhat abridged Winter Season centered around Christmas and New Year's Day then followed by somewhat of a lull until March and April. The big season for the Panhandle is the Summer Season.

—— *Florida Traffic Patterns* ——

Attraction touring takes place both while traveling en route and at the tourist's vacation destination. Southern Florida is a destination area; tourists, upon arrival, visit local attractions as a supplement to their vacation itinerary. The Orlando area is both a vacation destination and an en route center of tourism. Many visitors spend their entire vacation in the Orlando area while others visit en route to or from southern Florida. Ocala by contrast is largely an en route center of tourism with most tourists stopping on their way to or from other destinations.

Since most tourists do their traveling to and from their vacation destination on weekends, it is possible to identify patterns of traffic which are useful in avoiding crowds. As an example, a Tennessee family whose primary destination is Walt Disney World may tour Silver Springs at Ocala en route. Departing Tennessee on Friday evening or Saturday morning places them at Silver Springs on Sunday, arriving in the Orlando area on Sunday evening. Since this is a very common itinerary, executed by thousands of tourists every week, a traffic pattern becomes discernible. Silver Springs will show its heaviest attendance on weekends. Walt Disney World, as a destination, will show large crowds on Monday, Tuesday, and Wednesday. Sea World, Circus World, and other Orlando area attractions will see heavier attendance from Wednesday through Friday when visitors, such as our Tennessee family, have finished seeing the Magic Kingdom and EPCOT Center and begin to explore other attractions nearby.

Because of the extended driving distance, the average length of stay in Florida is greater for most tourists whose ultimate destination is southern Florida. An Ohio couple departing Columbus on Friday evening might typically tour St. Augustine or Marineland on Sunday and then proceed directly to their Fort Lauderdale destination or stop again for a day or two to tour Orlando area attractions. This itinerary places the couple at their Fort Lauderdale destination sometime late Monday, Tuesday, or Wednesday. Thus in southern Florida, attraction attendance is heaviest toward the end of the week, and as noted above, since visitors to southern Florida stay longer on the average, attendance remains heavy on weekends.

Thus, by understanding the more common patterns of arrival, departure, en route touring, and destination touring, it is possible to plan an attraction visitation itinerary which operates counter to the usual

Visitation patterns of specific centers of Florida Tourism

Area	Tourism Classification	Heaviest Attendance	When to Go
Panhandle	Destination	Weekends	Weekdays
St. Augustine, Marineland	En route	Weekends	Weekdays
Ocala	En route	Weekends	Weekdays
Weeki Wachee, Homosassa Springs	En route	Weekends	Weekdays
Orlando, Cape Kennedy	En route, Destination	Weekdays	Weekends
Tampa	En route, day trip from Orlando and from beaches	Thursday through Sunday	Monday through Wednesday
Clearwater, St. Petersburg	Destination	Winter: Sunday through Tuesday	Wednesday through Saturday
		Summer: Friday through Sunday	Monday through Thursday
Sarasota	En route, Destination, day trip from beaches to the north	Varies	Varies
Naples, Bonita Springs	Destination	Varies	Varies
Southern Florida, East Coast	Destination	Thursday through Sunday	Monday through Wednesday
Keys, Key West	Destination, day trip from beaches to the north	Weekdays	Weekends

traffic flow and places the tourist at each chosen attraction on a day of lighter attendance.

Displayed above in summary form is a guide to the visitation patterns of specific centers of Florida tourism. Note that light and heavy attendance are relative terms, with light attendance in season possibly exceeding heaviest attendance out of season. Also remember that traffic patterns described are based on the norm, and that a specific day, according to the law of averages, will probably but not necessarily, approximate the norm.

—— *When to Go to Walt Disney World* ——

Selecting the Time of Year for Your Visit

Walt Disney World is busiest of all Christmas Day through New Year's Day. Thanksgiving weekend, the week of Washington's Birthday, spring break for colleges, and the two weeks around Easter are also extremely busy. To give you some idea of what busy means at Walt Disney World, up to 92,000 people have toured the Magic Kingdom alone on a single day! While this level of attendance is far from typical, the possibility of its occurrence should forewarn all but the ignorant and the foolish from challenging this mega-attraction at its busiest periods.

The least busy time of all is from after the Thanksgiving weekend until the week before Christmas. The next slowest times are September through the weekend preceding Thanksgiving, January 4th through the first half of February, and the week following Easter through early June. At the risk of being blasphemous, our research team was so impressed with the relative ease of touring in the fall and other "off" periods that we would rather take our children out of school for a week than to do battle with the summer crowds.

Selecting the Day of the Week for Your Visit

The busiest days of the week are Monday through Thursday, with attendance tapering off slightly towards Thursday. Friday is the slowest day of the week, followed by Sunday. Saturday tends to be busy in the fall but is generally slack during the summer.

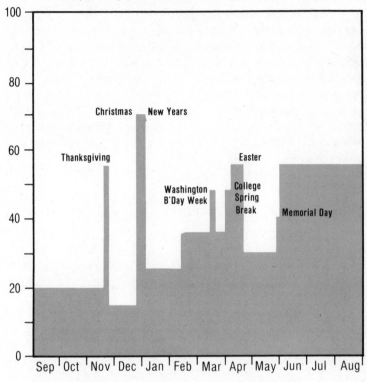

Visitors per Day per Park (thousands)

(Attendance figures represent weekly averages.)

—— *Packed Park Compensation Plan* ——

The thought of teeming, jostling throngs jockeying for position in endless lines under the baking Fourth of July sun is enough to wilt the will and ears of the most ardent Mouseketeer. Why would anyone go to Walt Disney World during a major holiday period? Indeed, if you have never been to Walt Disney World, and you thought you would just drop in for a few rides and a little look-see on such a day, you might be better off shooting yourself in the foot. The Disney folks, however, being Disney folks, feel kind of bad about those long, long lines and the basically impossible touring conditions on packed days and compensate their patrons with a no-less-than-incredible array of first-rate live entertainment and happenings.

Throughout the day the party goes on with shows, parades, concerts, and pageantry. In the evening, particularly, there is so much going on that you have to make some tough choices. There are concerts, parades, light shows, laser shows, fireworks, and dance occurring almost continually in both parks. No question about it, you can go to Walt Disney World on the Fourth of July (or on any other extended hours, crowded day), never get on a ride, and still get your money's worth five times over. Admittedly, it's not the ideal situation for a first-timer who really wants to see the theme parks, but for anyone else it's one heck of a good party.

A Word About Lodging

While this guide is not about lodging, we have found lodging to be a primary concern of those visiting Walt Disney World. Rooms in the Disney Theme Resort Hotels (Contemporary Resort Hotel, Polynesian Village, Golf Resort Hotel) are the most expensive; rooms at the Lake Buena Vista hotels (Walt Disney World Village) are next; and rooms at motels outside Walt Disney World are the least expensive. In addition to proximity and a certain number of guest privileges, the resort properties offer the special magic of staying inside Walt Disney World, and many visitors find the benefits worth the extra cost.

There is no real hardship, however, to staying outside Walt Disney World and driving (or taking the often available hotel shuttle) to the main gate for your visit. Meals can be had less expensively, too, and there is this indirect benefit: Rooming outside "The World" puts you in a more receptive mood towards other Orlando area attractions and eating establishments. Circus World, Cypress Gardens, and Sea World, among others, are well worth your attention.

Prices for accommodations are subject to change, but our research team lodged in an excellent (though not plush) motel surrounded by beautiful orange groves for one-quarter of the cost of staying in Walt Disney World. Our commuting time was seventeen minutes one way to the Magic Kingdom or EPCOT Center parking lots.

Travel Agents and Walt Disney World

Be advised that Walt Disney World does not give commissions to travel agents. This is significant to you for the following reasons: (1) your travel agent has no clout at Walt Disney World, so he cannot obtain special rates or packages as he may be able to elsewhere; and (2) since he obtains no commission, he may try to talk you out of staying in a Walt Disney World hotel.

Getting There

Directions

If you arrive by automobile you can reach the Magic Kingdom, EPCOT Center, the Theme Resort Hotels, the Fort Wilderness Campground, Discovery Island, and River Country via World Drive off US 192 or via EPCOT Center Drive off I-4 (see map, page 23).

If you are traveling *south* on the Florida Turnpike: Exit at Clermont, take US 27 south, turn left onto US 192, and then follow the signs to Walt Disney World.

If you are traveling *north* on the Florida Turnpike: Exit westbound onto I-4 and exit I-4 at EPCOT Center Drive.

If you are traveling *west* on I-4: Exit at EPCOT Center Drive and follow the signs.

If you are traveling *east* on I-4: Exit to US 192 northbound and then follow the signs.

Walt Disney World Village has its own entrance separate and distinct from entrances to the theme parks. To reach Walt Disney World Village take FL 535 exit off of I-4 and proceed north, following the signs.

The Parking Situation

The Magic Kingdom and EPCOT Center have their own pay parking lots (each one the size of Vermont), including close-in parking for the handicapped. In the case of the Magic Kingdom, a tram meets you at a loading station near where you parked and transports you to the Transportation and Ticket Center. Here you can buy passes to both the Magic Kingdom and EPCOT Center. If you wish to proceed to the Magic Kingdom you can either ride the ferryboat across Seven Seas Lagoon or catch the monorail. If you wish to go to EPCOT Center, you can board a separate monorail that connects EPCOT Center to

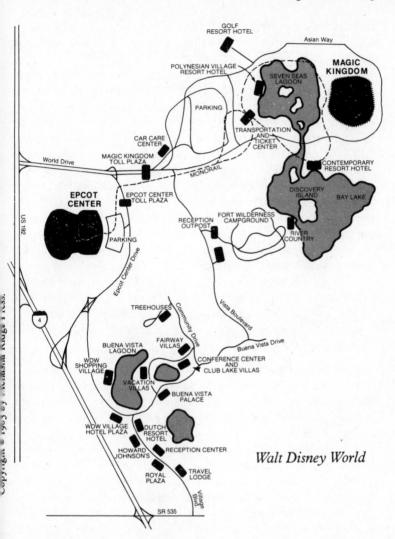

GOLF
RESORT HOTEL

Asian Way

POLYNESIAN VILLAGE
RESORT HOTEL

**MAGIC
KINGDOM**

SEVEN SEAS
LAGOON

PARKING

CAR CARE
CENTER

TRANSPORTATION
AND
TICKET
CENTER

MAGIC KINGDOM
TOLL PLAZA

World Drive

MONORAIL

CONTEMPORARY
RESORT HOTEL

**EPCOT
CENTER**

EPCOT CENTER
TOLL PLAZA

DISCOVERY
ISLAND

BAY LAKE

US 192

PARKING

RECEPTION
OUTPOST

FORT WILDERNESS
CAMPGROUND

RIVER
COUNTRY

4

TREEHOUSES

Community Drive

Vista Boulevard

Epcot Center Drive

BUENA VISTA
LAGOON

FAIRWAY
VILLAS

Buena Vista Drive

WDW
SHOPPING
VILLAGE

CONFERENCE CENTER
AND
CLUB LAKE VILLAS

VACATION
VILLAS

BUENA VISTA
PALACE

WDW VILLAGE
HOTEL PLAZA

DUTCH
RESORT
HOTEL

HOWARD
JOHNSON'S

RECEPTION CENTER

Walt Disney World

ROYAL
PLAZA

TRAVEL
LODGE

Village Blvd

SR 535

the Transportation and Ticket Center. The various sections of the
Magic Kingdom (Transportation and Ticket Center) parking lot are
named for Disney characters. Guests are given a receipt with a map of
the parking lot on the reverse side. Mark where you have parked on
the map and jot down the aisle number in the space provided. Put the
receipt in your billfold or some other safe place for referral when you

return to your car. Failure to take these precautions will often result in a lengthy search for your car at a time when you will be pretty tuckered out.

If you wish to visit EPCOT Center you can park at the Magic Kingdom (Transportation and Ticket Center) parking lot and commute via monorail, or park directly in the EPCOT Center parking lot. Arrangements in the EPCOT Center lot are essentially the same as described above; a tram will shuttle you from where you park to the EPCOT Center entrance, and you will be given a receipt/map where you can mark your parking place for later reference. At EPCOT Center the sections of the parking lot are named for pavilions in the Future World area of the park. The big difference between parking for the Magic Kingdom and parking for EPCOT Center is that access to the park is direct from the tram at EPCOT Center whereas to reach the Magic Kingdom you must transfer from the tram to the ferryboat or the monorail at the Transportation and Ticket Center. If you park at EPCOT Center and wish to go to the Magic Kingdom you may do so by taking the monorail from EPCOT Center to the Transportation and Ticket Center and then transferring to a Magic Kingdom monorail.

Taking a Tram or Shuttle Bus from Your Hotel

Trams and shuttle buses are provided by many hotels and motels in the vicinity of Walt Disney World. They represent a fairly carefree alternative for getting to and from the theme parks, letting you off right at the entrance and saving you the cost of parking. The rub is that they might not get you there as early as you desire (a critical point if you take our touring advice) or be available at the time you wish to return to your lodging. Also some shuttles go directly to Walt Disney World while others make stops at other motels and hotels in the vicinity. Each shuttle service is a little bit different so check out the particulars when you arrive at your hotel.

Making the Most of Your Time

Allocating Time

The Disney people recommend a day and a half to two full days at both the Magic Kingdom and EPCOT Center, or a total of three to four days for both attractions. While this may seem a little self-serving, it is not without basis. Both theme parks are HUGE, both require a lot of walking, and sometimes a lot of waiting in lines. Moving in and among typically large crowds all day is exhausting. Oftentimes, the unrelenting central Florida sun zaps the most hardy traveler, making tempers short. In our many visits to Walt Disney World we observed, particularly on hot summer days, a dramatic transition from happy, enthusiastic tourists upon arrival to zombies plodding along later in the day. Visitors who began their day enjoying the wonders of Disney imagination ultimately lapsed into an exhausted production mentality ("We've got two more rides in Fantasyland, then we can go back to the hotel").

Walt Disney World Admission Options

There are basically two Walt Disney World admission options:

1. 1-Day Tickets
2. World Passports (3, 4, 5-Day and one year)

The 1-Day Magic Kingdom or EPCOT Center Ticket is good for one-day admission and unlimited use of "attractions and experiences" at *either* the Magic Kingdom *or* EPCOT Center, but does not provide same-day admission to both.

World Passports "entitle the visitor to admission plus unlimited use of attractions and experiences at *both* the Magic Kingdom and EPCOT Center. Includes transportation between all Vacation Kingdom resort areas. World Passports need not be used on consecutive days." The 3-Day World Passport is a little over twice the cost of a 1-Day Ticket, and a 4-Day World Passport runs almost exactly three times the price of the 1-Day Ticket.

If you only have one day to spend, choose the park that most interests you and buy the 1-Day Ticket. If you have two days, go ahead and get the 3-Day World Passport. For the extra couple of dollars you can visit both parks on each day if you wish (as opposed to spending a whole day in each park respectively). At certain times of the year this will enable you to get in several extra hours of touring since the parks do not always close at the same time. You also will have unlimited use of the Monorail System.

If you plan to spend three days or more in the area, buy the 3, 4, or 5-Day World Passports. Remember, the passports do not have to be used on consecutive days. See our Optimum Touring Situation, below, for a relaxing, easygoing touring plan which makes use of this feature.

Which Park to See First: The Magic Kingdom or EPCOT Center?

This question is less academic than it appears at first glance, especially if there are children or teenagers in your party. Children who see the Magic Kingdom first expect more of the same type of entertainment at EPCOT Center and are often disappointed by its educational orientation and more serious tone. In fact, many adults react exactly the same way.

For first-time visitors especially, see EPCOT Center first; you will be able to enjoy it fully without having been preconditioned to thinking of Disney entertainment as solely in the fantasy/adventure genre. Parties which include children should definitely see EPCOT Center first. Children will be more likely to judge and enjoy EPCOT Center according to its own merits if they see it first, as well as being more relaxed and patient in their touring.

—— Optimum Touring Situation ——

The optimum touring situation would call for having four days of touring time at your disposal. Buy the "4-Day World Passport." It entitles you to admission plus unlimited use of attractions and experiences at both the Magic Kingdom and EPCOT Center and does not have to be used on consecutive days.

Day One: Arrive at the EPCOT Center main parking lot forty-five minutes before the stated opening time. Line up at the turnstile to be admitted as soon as the park opens. When the gates open proceed posthaste to the Spaceship Earth attraction at the base of the giant geodesic dome (if you do not arrive before the gates open, bypass this attraction for the time being). If a sit-down lunch or dinner at a World Showcase restaurant is among your top priorities, save Spaceship Earth for later and go directly to one of the WorldKey Information touch-sensitive video screens (located directly across the lobby from the Spaceship Earth exit ramp) and make lunch and/or dinner reservations at the World Showcase restaurant of your choice. (See the descriptive text in the section on EPCOT Center for detailed information about EPCOT Center attractions and use of the WorldKey Information Service.)

After making lunch and/or dinner reservations tour The Land pavilion and then the Journey into Imagination pavilion. Eat as per your lunch reservations and then exit EPCOT Center for an afternoon of relaxing or whatever tickles your fancy. In the early evening return refreshed to EPCOT Center to eat dinner and to tour the remainder of the Future World section of the park.

Day Two: Arrive early and make dining reservations as on Day 1 if you wish to try additional World Showcase or Future World restaurants. Tour as tastes dictate in Future World, progressing to the World Showcase section of the park when it opens at 10 A.M. Follow World Showcase Descriptions and Touring Tips, pages 126–31. Finish touring and browse the shops in the early afternoon, or, if you make dinner reservations, exit EPCOT Center and tour Discovery Island, or take the afternoon off, returning at the appointed time for dinner.

Day Three: Tour the Magic Kingdom early in the morning when the lines are short and the day is cooler. At about noon go back to your hotel for lunch and maybe a swim or a nap, whatever you feel like.

If the Magic Kingdom closes early (6 P.M.–8 P.M.), return refreshed about two hours before closing and continue your visit in the relative cool and diminished crowds of the evening. Eat dinner somewhere outside of Walt Disney World after the Magic Kingdom closes, or if you still have some energy, ride the monorail over to EPCOT Center which almost always stays open later.

If the Magic Kingdom closes late (9 P.M.–1 A.M.), eat a relaxed dinner outside Walt Disney World and return refreshed to enjoy the Magic Kingdom until closing time.

Day Four: Finish touring the Magic Kingdom in the early morning. At about noon take the monorail to the Contemporary Resort Hotel for lunch. Return to the Magic Kingdom to browse the shops and take in the Disney character parades and other live shows which are performed in the early and mid-afternoon, and which require no waiting in line.

Try to complete your visit about four o'clock and head back to your hotel for happy hour and a little rest. Check before leaving the Magic Kingdom to see if there will be an evening performance of the Electrical Water Pageant on the Seven Seas Lagoon. If the answer is yes (and it usually will be), head for the dock at the Polynesian Village at the appointed time (just after dusk) for uncrowded enjoyment of the show. If you are an early diner, grab a bite outside Walt Disney World before returning for the Electrical Water Pageant. If you like a late dinner, indulge your palate after the show.

The essence of the preceding Optimum Touring Situation is to see the various attractions of Walt Disney World in a series of shorter, less exhausting visits during the cooler, less crowded parts of the day, with plenty of rest and relaxation in between visits. Since the Optimum Touring Situation calls for exiting and returning to the theme parks on most days it obviously makes for easier logistics if you are staying in or fairly close to Walt Disney World (twenty miles or less to your hotel). If you are lodged too far away for a great deal of coming and going, try relaxing during the heat of the day in the lounges or on the waterfronts of the Resort Hotels, or alternatively, bring your swimming suit and spend an afternoon at River Country.

— *Seeing Walt Disney World on a Tight Schedule* —

Many visitors do not have four days to devote to Disney attractions. Some are en route to other Florida destinations while others wish to spend time sampling other central Florida attractions. For these visitors, efficient, time-effective touring is a must. They cannot afford long waits in line for rides, shows, or meals.

Even the most efficient touring plan will not allow the visitor to cover both the Magic Kingdom and EPCOT Center in one day, so plan on allocating at least an entire day to each attraction (an exception to this rule is when the theme parks close at different times, allowing the visitor to tour one park until closing time and then proceed to the other park). If your schedule only permits one day of touring overall, we recommend concentrating your efforts on only one of the theme parks and saving the other for a subsequent visit.

One-Day Touring

A comprehensive tour of the Magic Kingdom or EPCOT Center in one day is possible but requires a knowledge of the park, good planning, and no small reserve of energy and endurance. One-day touring does not leave much time for leisurely meals in sit-down restaurants, prolonged browsing in the many shops, or lengthy rest periods. Even so, one-day touring can be a fun, rewarding experience.

Successful one-day touring of either the Magic Kingdom or EPCOT Center hinges on THREE CARDINAL RULES:

Determine in Advance What You Really Want to See

What are the rides and attractions that appeal to you most? Which additional rides and attractions would you like to experience if you have any time left? What are you willing to forego?

Arrive Early! Arrive Early! Arrive Early!

This is the single most important key to efficient touring and avoiding long lines. First thing in the morning there are no lines and relatively few people. The same four rides which you can experience in one hour in the early morning will take more than three hours to see after 11:30 A.M. Have breakfast before you arrive so you will not have to waste your prime touring time sitting in a restaurant.

Always call the park, (305) 824-4321, the day before you visit to inquire at what time the park will open and close.

For the Magic Kingdom: Arrive at the main parking lot an hour and fifteen minutes before the stated opening time of the park (the parking lot and Transportation and Ticket Center open two hours early), buy your admission pass and take the monorail to the Magic Kingdom. You will find that Main Street, U.S.A. opens an hour before the stated opening time of the park. Tour Main Street and be ready to see the other theme areas when they open.

For EPCOT Center: Arrive at the main parking lot forty-five minutes before the stated opening time. Buy your admission pass and line up at the turnstile to be admitted as soon as the park opens. EPCOT Center sometimes opens a half hour earlier than the stated opening time.

Avoid Bottlenecks

Helping you avoid bottlenecks is what this guide is all about. Bottlenecks occur as a result of crowd concentrations and/or less than optimal crowd management. Concentrations of hungry people create bottlenecks at restaurants during the lunch and dinner hours; concentrations of people moving towards the exit near closing time create bottlenecks in the gift shops en route to the gate; concentrations of visitors at new and unusually popular rides create bottlenecks and long waiting lines; rides which are slow in boarding and disembarking passengers create bottlenecks and long waiting lines. Avoiding bottlenecks involves being able to predict where, when, and why they occur. To this end we provide **Touring Plans** for both EPCOT Center and the Magic Kingdom to assist you in avoiding bottlenecks. In addition we provide detailed information on all rides and performances which allows you to estimate how long you may have to wait in line, and it also allows you to compare rides in terms of their capacity to accommodate large crowds. Touring plans for the Magic Kingdom begin on page 88; touring plans for EPCOT Center begin on page 151.

— *Touring Plans: What They Are and How They Work* —

When we interviewed Walt Disney World visitors who toured the theme park on slow days, say in early December, they invariably waxed eloquent about the sheer delight of their experience. When we questioned visitors, however, who toured on a moderate or busy day, they spent much of the interview telling us about the jostling crowds and how much time they stood in line. What a shame, they said, that you should devote so much time and energy to fighting the crowds in a place as special as Walt Disney World.

Given this complaint, we descended on Walt Disney World with a team of researchers to determine whether a touring plan could be devised that would move the visitor counter to the flow of traffic and allow him to see virtually all of either the Magic Kingdom or EPCOT Center in one day with only minimal waits in line. On some of the busiest days of the year, our team monitored traffic flow into and through the theme parks, noting how the parks filled and how the patrons were distributed among the various attractions. Likewise, we observed which rides and attractions were most popular and where bottlenecks were most likely to form.

After many long days of collecting data, we devised a number of preliminary touring plans which we tested during one of the busiest weeks of the entire year. Each day individual members of our research team would tour the park according to one of the preliminary plans, noting how long it took to walk from place to place and how long the wait in line was for each ride or show. Combining the knowledge gained through these trial runs, we devised a master plan which we retested and fine-tuned. This plan, with very little variance from day to day, allowed us to experience all of the major rides and attractions, and most of the lesser ones, in one day, with an average wait in line at each ride or show of less than five minutes.

From this master plan we developed a number of alternative plans that take into account the varying tastes and personal requirements of different Walt Disney World patrons. We devised a plan, for instance, for more mature guests that bypasses roller-coaster-type rides and requires less walking. Another plan was assembled for parents touring with children under the age of eight years. Each plan operates with the same efficiency as the master plan but addresses the special needs and preferences of its intended users.

Finally, after all of the plans were tested by our staff, we selected (using convenience sampling) a number of everyday Walt Disney World patrons to test the plans. The only prerequisite for being chosen for the test group (the visitors who would test the touring plans) was that the guest must be visiting a Disney attraction for the first time. A second group of ordinary patrons was chosen for a "control group," first-time visitors who would tour the park according to their own plans but who would make notes of what they did and how much time they spent waiting in lines.

When the two groups were compared, the results proved no less than amazing. On days when each park's attendance exceeded 48,000, visitors touring on their own (without the plan) **averaged** 3⅔ hours more waiting in line per day than the patrons touring according to our plan, and they experienced 37 percent fewer rides and attractions.

Will the Plans Continue to Work Once the Secret Is Out?

Yes! First, all of the plans require that a patron be on hand when the theme parks open. Many vacationers simply refuse to make this early-rising sacrifice, but you can see more in the one hour just after the parks open than in several hours once the parks begin to fill. Second, it is anticipated that less than 1 percent of any given day's attendance will have been exposed to the plans, not enough to bias the results. Last, most groups will interpret the plans somewhat, skipping certain rides or shows as a matter of personal taste.

Variables That Will Affect the Success of the Touring Plans

How quickly you move from one ride to another, when and how many refreshment and restroom breaks you take, when, where, and how you eat meals, and your ability (or lack thereof) to find your way around will all have an impact on the success of the plans. We recommend continuous, expeditious touring until around 11:30 A.M. After that hour, breaks and so on will not affect the plans significantly.

General Overview

The Walt Disney World Touring Plans are step-by-step plans for seeing as much as possible in one day with a minimum of time wasted standing in line. They are designed to assist you in avoiding crowds and bottlenecks on days of moderate to heavy attendance. On days of lighter attendance (see "Selecting the Time of Year for Your Visit," page 18), the plans will still save you time but will not be as critical to successful touring.

PART TWO—Tips and Warnings

—— Credit Cards ——

— MasterCard and American Express are accepted for theme park admission.
— No credit cards are accepted in the theme parks at fast-food restaurants.
— VISA is *not* accepted anywhere for any purpose in all of Walt Disney World (there must be a good story behind this fact somewhere).
— Walt Disney World shops, sit-down restaurants, and Theme Resort Hotels will accept American Express and MasterCard credit cards only.

—— Rain ——

If it rains go anyway; the bad weather will serve to diminish the crowds. Additionally, most of the rides and attractions in both the Magic Kingdom and EPCOT Center are under cover. Likewise, in both theme parks, all but a few of the waiting areas are protected from inclement weather.

—— Small Children ——

We believe that children should be a fairly mature eight years old to really *appreciate* the Magic Kingdom, though children of almost any age will *enjoy* it.

We believe that much of value at EPCOT Center will be lost on children less than ten years old, although children five years and older will be able to enjoy many specific features.

Small children often become tired and irritable after several hours of standing in line and being jostled among the crowds. If your schedule allows, we recommend small doses at a time of both the Magic Kingdom and EPCOT Center. Go early in the morning to the park of your choice and tour until about lunch time. Go back to your hotel for some food and maybe a nap. Return later in the evening or the morning of the following day.

Strollers—are available for rent at a modest fee at both theme parks. For infants and nonwalking toddlers the strollers are a must. We observed several sharp parents renting strollers for somewhat older children (up to 4 or 5 years). Having the stroller precluded having to carry children when they ran out of steam, and also afforded a place for children to sit during long waits in line. Strollers can be obtained at the right of the entrance to the Magic Kingdom (at the base of the Main Street Station) and on the left side of the Entrance Plaza of EPCOT Center.

NOTE: Sometimes strollers disappear while you are enjoying a ride or a show. Do not be alarmed. You will not have to buy the missing stroller and you will be issued a new stroller for your continued use.

Baby-Sitting. If you are staying in one of the Theme Resort Hotels, you can contract for a baby-sitter to watch the kids in your hotel room. If you are staying anywhere on Walt Disney World property, including the Fort Wilderness Campground or the non-Disney-owned hotels at Walt Disney World Village, you can arrange for your children to be cared for at the Kindercare facility located at the Walt Disney World Village. For rates and other vital information call (305) 827-5437. Many of the larger motels and hotels outside of Walt Disney World also offer some sort of baby-sitting service; inquire when you make your reservations.

Caring for Infants and Toddlers. Both the Magic Kingdom and EPCOT Center have special centralized facilities for the care of infants and toddlers. Everything necessary for changing diapers, preparing formulas, warming bottles and food, etc., is available in ample quantity. A broad selection of baby supplies is on hand for sale and there are even rockers and special chairs for nursing mothers. In the Magic Kingdom the Baby Center is located next to the Crystal Palace at the end of Main Street. At EPCOT Center, Baby Services is located near the Odyssey Restaurant, situated to the right of the World of Motion in Future World.

Lost Children—normally do not present much of a problem at either theme park. All Disney employees are schooled to handle the situation should it be encountered. If you lose a child in the Magic Kingdom, report the situation to a Disney employee, and then check in at the Baby Center and at City Hall where lost children "logs" are maintained. At EPCOT Center the procedure is the same; report the child lost and then check at Baby Services near the Odyssey Restaurant. There are no paging systems in either park, but in an emergency an "all points bulletin" can be issued throughout the park(s) via internal communications. At both theme parks, special name tags can be obtained to aid identification should a child become separated from his party.

Disney, Kids, and Scary Stuff. Disney rides and shows are adventures. They focus on the substance and themes of all adventure, and indeed of life itself: good and evil, quest, death, beauty and the grotesque, fellowship and enmity. As you sample the variety of attractions at Walt Disney World, you transcend the mundane spinning and bouncing of midway rides to a more thought-provoking and emotionally powerful entertainment experience. Though the endings are all happy, the impact of the adventures, with Disney's gift for special effects, is often intimidating and occasionally frightening to small children.

There are rides with menacing witches, rides with burning towns, and rides with ghouls popping out of their graves, all done tongue-in-cheek and with a sense of humor, providing you are old enough to understand the joke. And bones, lot of bones: human bones, cattle bones, dinosaur bones, and whole skeletons everywhere you look. There have got to be more bones at Walt Disney World than at the Smithsonian Institute and Tulane Medical School combined. There is a stack of skulls at the headhunter's camp on the Jungle Cruise; a veritable platoon of skeletons sailing ghost ships in Pirates of the Caribbean; a haunting assemblage of skulls and skeletons in the Haunted Mansion; and more skulls, skeletons, and bones punctuating Snow White's Scary Adventure, Peter Pan's Flight, and Big Thunder Mountain Railroad, to name a few.

Most small children take Disney's variety of macabre trappings in stride, and others are quickly comforted by an arm around the shoulder or a little squeeze of the hand. But for those kids whose parents have observed a tendency to become upset when exposed to such sights, we recommend taking it slow and easy, sampling more benign adventures like the Jungle Cruise, gauging reactions, and discussing with children how they felt about the things they saw.

—— *Visitors with Special Needs* ——

Handicapped visitors—will find rental wheelchairs available if needed. Most rides, shows, attractions, restrooms, and restaurants at both theme parks are designed to accommodate the handicapped. For specific inquiries or problems call (305) 824-4321. If you are in the Magic Kingdom and need some special assistance go to City Hall on Main Street. At EPCOT Center inquire at the Guest Relations booth in the base of Earth Station in Future World. There is also a Guest Relations window at the Transportation and Ticket Center.

Close-in parking is available for handicapped visitors at both the EPCOT Center parking complex and at the Ticket and Transportation Center. Simply request directions when you pay your parking fee upon entering. All monorails and most rides, shows, restrooms, and restaurants can accommodate wheelchairs. One major exception is the Contemporary Resort Hotel monorail station where passengers must enter or exit via escalators.

A special information booklet for handicapped guests is available at wheelchair rental locations in both parks, at City Hall in the Magic Kingdom and at Earth Station in EPCOT Center.

Foreign language assistance—is available throughout Walt Disney World. Inquire by calling (305) 824-4321 or by stopping in at City Hall in the Magic Kingdom or at Guest Relations in Earth Station at EPCOT Center.

Messages—can be left at City Hall in the Magic Kingdom or at Guest Relations in Earth Station at EPCOT Center.

Car Trouble. If your car goes on the fritz, the Disney Car Care Center will come to the rescue. Arrangements can be made for transportation to your Walt Disney World destination and for a lift to the Car Care Center. If the problem is simple, one of the security or tow truck patrols which continually cruise the parking lots might be able to put you back in business.

Lost and Found. If you lose (or find) something in the Magic Kingdom, City Hall (once again) is the place to go. At EPCOT Center the Lost and Found is located in the Entrance Plaza. If you do not discover your loss until you have left the park(s), call (305) 824-4245 (both theme parks).

— *Excuse Me, but Where Can I Find . . .* —

Someplace to Put All These Packages?   Lockers are available on the ground floor of the Main Street Railroad Station in the Magic Kingdom, to the right of Earth Station in EPCOT Center, and on both the east and west ends of the Ticket and Transportation Center.

A Mixed Drink or a Beer?   If you are in the Magic Kingdom you are out of luck. You will have to exit the park and proceed to one of the Resort Hotels. In EPCOT Center you can have a drink, but you may need a reservation. Alcoholic beverages are served primarily in full-service eateries, although beer is available at the Cantina de San Angel opposite the Mexican pavilion; at Le Cellier, a cafeteria on the lower right side of the Canadian pavilion; and at the pub section of the Rose and Pub Dining Room in the Great Britain complex. The latter is popular not only because of the availability of beer, but also because of its unparalleled view of the World Showcase Lagoon. Finally, beer is also available at Yakatori House, the fast-food eatery in the Japanese pavilion.

Some Rain Gear?   If you get caught in a central Florida monsoon, here's where you can find something to cover up with:

Magic Kingdom	
Main Street:	The Emporium
Tomorrowland:	Mickey's Mart
Fantasyland:	Mad Hatter
	AristoCats
Frontierland:	Frontier Trading Post
Adventureland:	Tropic Toppers
EPCOT Center:	Almost all retail shops

A Cure for This Headache?   Aspirin and various other sundries can be purchased on Main Street in the Magic Kingdom at the Emporium (they keep them behind the counter so you have to ask), at most retail outlets in EPCOT Center Future World, and in many of the World Showcase shops.

ca段

A Prescription Filled?   Unfortunately there is no place in either the Magic Kingdom or EPCOT Center to have a prescription filled. In fact, as of this writing, the nearest pharmacy is situated on US 192 in Kissimmee, almost 12 miles distant.

Suntan Lotion?   Suntan lotion and various other sundries can be purchased on Main Street in the Magic Kingdom at the Emporium (they keep them behind the counter so you have to ask), at most retail outlets in EPCOT Center Future World, and in many of the World Showcase shops.

A Smoke?   Cigarettes are readily available throughout both the Magic Kingdom and EPCOT Center.

> ### Magic Kingdom
> | | |
> |---|---|
> | Main Street: | The Tobacconist |
> | Tomorrowland: | Mickey's Mart |
> | Fantasyland: | Royal Candy Shop |
> | | King Stefan's in Cinderella Castle (vending machine) |
> | | Pinocchio Village Haus (vending machine) |
> | Liberty Square: | Columbia Harbor House (vending machine) |
> | | Heritage House |
> | Frontierland: | Frontier Trading Post |
> | | Mile Long Bar (vending machine) |
> | Adventureland: | Tropic Toppers |
>
> **EPCOT Center**   Cigarettes are available at most Future World retail outlets and can be located in at least one of the shops in each of the World Showcase pavilions. Special imported cigarettes are additionally available at the British, French, and German pavilions.

Feminine Hygiene Products?   Feminine hygiene products are available in most of the women's restrooms in both the Magic Kingdom and EPCOT Center.

Cash?   A branch of the Sun Bank is located on Main Street in the Magic Kingdom and to the left of the turnstiles as you enter EPCOT Center. Both branches offer the following services:

— *Provide cash advances on MasterCard and VISA* credit cards ($50 minimum with a maximum equaling the patron's credit limit).

— *Cash personal checks* of $25 and less drawn on US banks upon presentation of a valid driver's license and a major credit card.

— *Cash and sell traveler's checks.* Provide refunds for lost American Express traveler's checks.

— *Facilitate the wiring of money* from the visitor's bank to the Sun Bank.

— *Exchange foreign currency* for dollars.

Exchange My Foreign Currency? The currency of most countries can be exchanged for dollars before entering the theme parks at the Guest Relations window of the Ticket and Transportation Center and at the Guest Relations window EPCOT Center (to the right of the entrance turnstiles). Once inside, foreign currency can be exchanged at the Sun Bank branch of either park.

Leave My Pet? Cooping up an animal in a hot car while you tour can lead to disastrous results. Additionally, pets are not allowed in the major or minor theme parks. Kennels and holding facilities are provided for the temporary care of your pets, and are located adjacent to the Transportation and Ticket Center and to the left of the EPCOT Center Entrance Plaza. If you are adamant, the folks at the kennels will accept custody of just about any type of animal, though owners of exotic and/or potentially vicious pets must place their charge in the assigned cage. Small pets (mice, hamsters, birds, snakes, turtles, alligators, etc.) must arrive in their own escape-proof quarters.

In addition to the above, there are several other details that you may need to know:

— Advance reservations for animals are not accepted.

— Kennels open one hour before the theme parks open and close one hour after the theme parks close.

— Only Walt Disney World Resort guests may board a pet overnight.

— Guests leaving exotic pets should supply food for their pet.

Film?   Camera centers are located near the Journey into Imagination pavilion and Spaceship Earth and at other shops throughout EPCOT Center. In the Magic Kingdom, film may be found at the Kodak Camera Center on Main Street, U.S.A., as well as at other shops throughout the park.

PART THREE—The Magic Kingdom

Arriving and Getting Oriented

Both the ferryboat and the monorail discharge passengers at the entrance to the Magic Kingdom—the Train Station at the foot of Main Street. Stroller and wheelchair rentals are to the right, lockers for your use are on the ground floor of the Train Station. Entering Main Street, City Hall is to your left, serving as the center for information, lost and found, some reservations, and entertainment.

If you haven't been given a guide to the Magic Kingdom by now, City Hall is the place to pick one up. The guide contains maps, gives tips for good photos, lists all the attractions, shops, and eating places, and provides helpful information about first aid, baby care, assistance for the handicapped, and more.

While at City Hall inquire about special events, live entertainment, Disney character parades, concerts, and other activities scheduled for that day. Sometimes City Hall will have a printed schedule of the day's events; other days no printed handouts are available and you will have to take a few notes.

Notice from your map that Main Street ends at a central hub from which branch the entrances to the other five sections of the Magic Kingdom: Adventureland, Frontierland, Liberty Square, Fantasyland, and Tomorrowland. Cinderella Castle serves as the entrance to Fantasyland and is the focal landmark and visual center of the Magic Kingdom. If you start in Adventureland and go clockwise around the Magic Kingdom, the castle spires will always be roughly on your right; if you start in Tomorrowland and go counterclockwise through the park, the spires will always be roughly on your left. Cinderella Castle is a great place to meet if your group decides to split up for any reason during the day, or as an emergency meeting place if you are accidentally separated.

Starting the Tour

Everyone will soon find his own favorite and not-so-favorite attractions in the Magic Kingdom. Be open-minded and adventuresome. Don't dismiss a particular ride or show as being not for you until **after** you have tried it. Our personal experience as well as our research indicates that each visitor is different in terms of which Disney offerings he most enjoys. So don't miss seeing an attraction because a friend from home didn't like it; that attraction may turn out to be your favorite.

We do recommend that you take advantage of what Disney does best—the fantasy adventures like the Jungle Cruise and the Haunted Mansion, and the Audio-Animatronics (talking robots, so to speak) attractions such as the Hall of Presidents and Pirates of the Caribbean. Unless you have almost unlimited time, don't burn a lot of daylight browsing through the shops. Except for some special Disney souvenirs, you can find most of the same merchandise elsewhere. Try to minimize the time you spend on carnival-type rides; you've probably got an amusement park, carnival, or state fair closer to your hometown. (Don't, however, mistake rides like Space Mountain and the Big Thunder Mountain Railroad as being amusement park rides. They may be of the roller coaster genre, but they represent pure Disney genius.) Similarly, do not devote a lot of time to waiting in lines for meals. Food at most Magic Kingdom eateries is mediocre and uninspiring at best. Eat a good early breakfast before you come and snack on vendor-sold foods during the touring day.

Main Street, U.S.A.

Main Street opens one hour before and closes one hour after the rest of the park. Since this situation essentially provides two extra hours of touring time, tour Main Street before the rest of the park opens, finishing up anything you missed in the morning during the extra hour Main Street is open in the evening.

This section of the Magic Kingdom is where you'll begin and end your visit. We have already mentioned that assistance and information are available at City Hall. The Walt Disney World Railroad stops at the Main Street Station: you can board here for a grand-circle tour of the Magic Kingdom, or you can get off the train in Frontierland.

Main Street is a replication of a turn-of-the-century American small town street. Many visitors are surprised to discover that all the buildings are real as opposed to being elaborate props. Attention to detail here is exceptional with interiors, furnishings, and fixtures conforming to the period. As with any real Main Street the Disney version is essentially a collection of shops and eating places, with a city hall, a fire station, an old-time cinema, and an attraction detailing the life of Walt Disney, *Walt Disney Story*, thrown in for good measure. Horsedrawn trolleys, double-decker buses, fire engines, and horseless carriages offer rides along Main Street and transport visitors to the central hub.

Walt Disney World Railroad

DESCRIPTION AND COMMENTS   Basically, a transportation ride.

TOURING TIPS   Save the train ride until after you have seen the featured attractions, or use when you need transportation.

Walt Disney Story

DESCRIPTION AND COMMENTS   A warm and well-produced remembrance of the man who started it all. Well worth seeing, especially touching for those old enough to remember Walt Disney.

TOURING TIPS   You usually do not have to wait long for this show, so see it during the busy times of the day when lines are long elsewhere or as you are leaving the park.

Main Street Cinema

DESCRIPTION AND COMMENTS   Excellent old-time movies, including some vintage Disney cartoons.

TOURING TIPS   Good place to get out of the sun or rain or to kill time while others in your group shop on Main Street; something you can afford to miss.

Main Street Shops and Restaurants

DESCRIPTION AND COMMENTS   Mediocre food; specialty/souvenir shopping in a nostalgic, happy setting.

TOURING TIPS   The shops are fun but the merchandise can be had elsewhere (except for certain Disney trademark souvenirs). If seeing the park attractions is your objective, save the Main Street eateries and shops until the end of the day. If shopping is your objective, you will find the shops most crowded during the noon hour and near closing time.

Main Street Vehicles

DESCRIPTION AND COMMENTS   Trolleys, buses, etc., which add color to Main Street.

TOURING TIPS   Will save you a walk to the central hub. Not worth waiting for in line.

Adventureland

Adventureland is the first land to the left of Main Street and combines a safari/African motif with an old New Orleans/Caribbean motif.

Swiss Family Island Treehouse

DESCRIPTION AND COMMENTS   A fantastic replication of the ship-wrecked family's home will fire the imagination of the inventive and the adventurous.

TOURING TIPS   A self-guided walk-through tour which involves a lot of climbing up and down stairs, but no ropes or ladders or anything fancy. People stopping during the walk-through to look extra long or to rest sometimes create bottlenecks which slow crowd flow. We recommend visiting this attraction in the late afternoon or early evening if you are on a one-day tour schedule, or first thing in the morning of your second day.

Jungle Cruise

DESCRIPTION AND COMMENTS   A boat ride through jungle waterways. Passengers encounter elephants, lions, hostile natives, and a menacing hippo. A long-enduring Disney favorite, with the boatman's spiel adding measurably to the fun.

TOURING TIPS   One of the park's "not to be missed" attractions. Go early; this ride loads slowly and long lines form as the park fills. Also, much of the waiting area is exposed to the elements.

Pirates of the Caribbean

DESCRIPTION AND COMMENTS   Another boat ride, this time indoors, through a series of sets depicting a pirate raid on an island settlement, from the bombardment of the fortress to the debauchery that follows the victory. All in good, clean fun.

TOURING TIPS   Another "not to be missed" attraction. Undoubtedly one of the most elaborate and imaginative attractions in the Magic Kingdom. Engineered to move large crowds in a hurry, Pirates is a good attraction to see during the busy middle part of the day. It has two waiting lines, both under cover (try the one on the left).

Tropical Serenade (Enchanted Tiki Birds)

DESCRIPTION AND COMMENTS   An unusual sit-down theater performance where more than two hundred birds, flowers, and Tiki-god statues sing and whistle through a musical program.

TOURING TIPS   One of the more bizarre of the Magic Kingdom's entertainments, but usually not too crowded. We like it in the late afternoon when we can especially appreciate sitting for a bit in an air-conditioned theater.

Adventureland Eateries and Shops

DESCRIPTION AND COMMENTS   More specialty shopping and mediocre food.

TOURING TIPS   Skip the shops and eateries unless you specifically came to shop and eat, or try them on your second day.

Frontierland

Frontierland adjoins Adventureland as you move clockwise around the Magic Kingdom. The focus here is on the Old West with stockade-type structures and pioneer trappings.

Big Thunder Mountain Railroad

DESCRIPTION AND COMMENTS   A roller coaster ride through and around a 200-foot mountain. The time is Gold Rush days, and the idea is that you are on a runaway mine train. Along with the usual thrills of a roller coaster ride (about a 7 on a "scary scale" of 10), the ride showcases some first-rate examples of Disney creativity: life-like scenes depicting a mining town, a flash flood, and an earthquake, all humorously peopled and animated.

TOURING TIPS   A superb Disney experience, but not too wild a roller coaster. The emphasis here is much more on the sights than on the thrill of the ride itself. Regardless, it's a "not to be missed" attraction. The best bet for riding Big Thunder without a long wait in line is to ride early in the morning.

Diamond Horseshoe Revue

DESCRIPTION AND COMMENTS   A half-hour, G-rated re-creation of an Old West dance hall show, with dancing, singing, and lots of corny comedy. Visitors are seated at tables where snacks and beverages (nonalcoholic) can be ordered before the show. This is a good performance, but you can see this sort of entertainment with far less effort elsewhere.

TOURING TIPS   Though we acknowledge the quality of the show, we recommend that this attraction be skipped unless you have two full days to devote to the Magic Kingdom. Here's why: Seating is by reservation only, made in person on the day you want to see the show. To obtain a reservation you have to run first thing in the morning to the Diamond Horseshoe Saloon and stand in line when you could be hopping on any ride you liked without much, if any, waiting. Reservation lines at the Saloon move very slowly because every visitor needs to ask questions and receive instructions. If you are able to obtain a reservation for one of the several shows you will be required to return for seating one-half hour before showtime when you will wait in line again (this time to be admitted to the theater). Once allowed inside you will wait for another fifteen minutes for food orders to be taken and processed before the show finally begins. By observation and experimentation we have determined that a Magic Kingdom visitor spends an average of one hour making his reservation, and forty-five minutes waiting for the show to begin, plus changing his other touring plans to get back to Frontierland in time to be seated. Thus, counting the show itself, a two-hour-and-fifteen-minute investment of valuable time to see a thirty-minute song-and-dance show.

Country Bear Jamboree

DESCRIPTION AND COMMENTS   A cast of charming AudioAnimatronics (robotic) bears sing and stomp their way through a Western-style hoedown. One of the Magic Kingdom's most humorous and upbeat shows.

TOURING TIPS   Yet another "not to be missed" attraction, the Jamboree is extremely popular and draws large crowds even early in the day. We recommend seeing this one before 11:30 A.M. If you arrive at the Jamboree in the park's early hours of operation and find that you have a few minutes' wait until the next show, you may be able to zip over for a quick ride on Big Thunder Mountain Railroad.

Tom Sawyer Island

DESCRIPTION AND COMMENTS   Tom Sawyer Island manages to impart something of a sense of isolation from the rest of the park. It has hills to climb, a cave and a windmill to explore, a tipsy barrel bridge to cross, and paths to follow. It's a delight for adults and a godsend for children who have been in tow all day. They love the freedom of the exploration and the excitement of firing air guns from the walls of Ft. Sam Clemens. There's even a "secret" escape tunnel.

TOURING TIPS   Tom Sawyer Island is not one of the Magic Kingdom's more celebrated attractions, but it's certainly one of the better done. Attention to detail is excellent and kids particularly revel in its adventuresome frontier atmosphere. We think it's a must for families with children five through fifteen. If your party is adult, visit the island on your second day or stop by on your first day if you have seen the attractions you most wanted to see.

We like Tom Sawyer Island from about noon until the island closes at dusk. Access is by raft from Frontierland and you will have to stand in line to board both coming and going. Two rafts operate simultaneously, however, and the round trip is usually pretty efficient. Tom Sawyer Island takes about forty-five minutes or so to see; many children could spend a whole day visiting.

Davy Crockett's Explorer Canoes

DESCRIPTION AND COMMENTS   Paddle-powered ride (your power) around Tom Sawyer Island and Ft. Sam Clemens. Runs the same route with the same sights as the Liberty Square Riverboat and the Mike Fink Keelboats. The canoes only operate during the busy times of the year. The sights are fun and the ride is a little different in that the tourists paddle the canoe.

TOURING TIPS   The canoes represent one of three ways to see the same territory. Since the canoes and keelboats are slower loading, we usually opt for the large riverboat. If you are not up for a boat ride, a different view of the same sights can be had hoofing around Tom Sawyer Island and Ft. Sam Clemens.

The Frontierland Shootin' Gallery

DESCRIPTION AND COMMENTS   A very elaborate shooting gallery where you can buy twelve bullets for about a quarter. One of the few attractions not included in the Magic Kingdom admission.

TOURING TIPS   Good fun for them "what likes to shoot," but definitely not a place to be blowing your time if you are on a tight schedule. Try it on your second day if time allows.

Walt Disney World Railroad

DESCRIPTION AND COMMENTS   Same railroad described in the Main Street section.

TOURING TIPS   Many times we end up in Frontierland around lunch time. If we are not on a tight schedule we catch the train back to Main Street, exit the Magic Kingdom, and take the monorail to the Contemporary Resort Hotel for lunch.

Frontierland Eateries and Shops

DESCRIPTION AND COMMENTS More specialty and souvenir shopping and undistinguished bulk food for the masses.

TOURING TIPS Don't waste time browsing shops or standing in line for food unless you have a very relaxed schedule or came specifically to shop.

Liberty Square

Liberty Square recreates the atmosphere of Colonial America at the time of the American Revolution. Architecture is Federal or Colonial, with a real 130-year-old live oak (dubbed the "Liberty Tree") lending dignity and grace to the setting.

Hall of Presidents

DESCRIPTION AND COMMENTS   A twenty-minute strongly inspirational and patriotic program highlighting milestones in American history. The performance climaxes with a roll call of presidents from Washington through the present, with a few words of encouragement from President Lincoln. A very moving show coupled with one of Disney's best and most ambitious Audio-Animatronics (robotic) efforts.

TOURING TIPS   Definitely a "not to be missed" attraction. The detail and costume of the chief executives is incredible, and if your children tend to fidget during the show, take notice of the fact that the Presidents do, too. This attraction is one of the most popular, particularly among older visitors, and draws large crowds from 11:00 A.M. through about 5:00 P.M. Do not be dismayed by the lines, however. The theater holds more than 700 people, thus swallowing up large lines at a single gulp when visitors are admitted. One show is always in progress while the lobby is being filled for the next show. At less than busy times you will probably be admitted directly to the lobby without waiting in line. When the waiting lobby fills, those remaining in line outside are held in place until those in the lobby move into the theater just prior to the next show, at which time another 700 people from the outside line are admitted to the lobby.

Liberty Square Riverboat

DESCRIPTION AND COMMENTS   Large-capacity paddle wheel riverboat that navigates the waters around Tom Sawyer Island and Ft. Sam

Clemens. A beautiful craft, the riverboat provides a lofty perspective of Frontierland and Liberty Square.

TOURING TIPS One of three boat rides that survey the same real estate. Since Davy Crockett's Explorer Canoes and the Mike Fink Keelboats are slower loading, we think the riverboat is the best bet. If you are not in the mood for a boat ride, much of the same sights can be seen by hiking around the island.

Haunted Mansion

DESCRIPTION AND COMMENTS A fun attraction more than a scary one with some of the best special effects in the Magic Kingdom. In their guidebook the Disney people say, "Come face to face with 999 happy ghosts, ghouls, and goblins in a 'frightfully funny' adventure." That pretty well sums it up. Be warned that some youngsters become overly anxious concerning what they think they will see. The actual attraction scares almost nobody.

TOURING TIPS This attraction would be more at home in Fantasyland, but no matter, it's Disney at its best; another "not to be missed" feature. Lines at the Haunted Mansion ebb and flow more than do the lines of most other Magic Kingdom high spots. This is due to the Mansion's proximity to the Hall of Presidents and the Liberty Square Riverboat. These two attractions disgorge 750 and 450 people respectively at one time every time they turn over. Many of these folks head right over and hop in line at the Haunted Mansion. Try this attraction before noon and after 4:30 P.M. and make an effort to slip in between crowds.

Mike Fink Keelboats

DESCRIPTION AND COMMENTS Small river keelboats which circle Tom Sawyer Island and Ft. Sam Clemens, taking the same route as Davy Crockett's Explorer Canoes and the Liberty Square Riverboat. The top deck of the keelboat is exposed to the elements.

TOURING TIPS This trip covers the same circle traveled by Davy Crockett's Explorer Canoes and the Liberty Square Riverboat. Since the keelboats and the canoes load slowly we prefer the riverboat. Another way to see much of the area covered by the respective boat tours is to explore Tom Sawyer Island and Ft. Sam Clemens on foot.

Liberty Square Eateries and Shops

DESCRIPTION AND COMMENTS   Specialty and souvenir shopping and typical Disney bland food, bulk-loading restaurants.

TOURING TIPS   Save the shops for another day unless you're on a shopping trip. If you're hungry grab a snack from a vendor.

Fantasyland

Truly an enchanting place, spread gracefully like a miniature Alpine village beneath the lofty towers of Cinderella Castle, Fantasyland is the heart of the Magic Kingdom.

It's a Small World

DESCRIPTION AND COMMENTS   A happy, upbeat attraction with a world brotherhood theme and a catchy tune that will roll around in your head for weeks. Small boats convey visitors on a tour around the world, with singing and dancing dolls showcasing the dress and culture of each nation. Almost everyone enjoys It's a Small World, but it stands, along with the *Enchanted Tiki Birds*, as an attraction that some could take or leave while others think it is one of the real masterpieces of the Magic Kingdom. We rank it as a "not to be missed" attraction. Try it and form your own opinion.

TOURING TIPS   A "not to be missed" attraction, It's a Small World is a fast-loading ride with two waiting lines—try the line on the left. Usually a good bet during the busier times of the day.

Skyway to Tomorrowland

DESCRIPTION AND COMMENTS   Part of the Magic Kingdom internal transportation system, the Skyway is a chairlift that conveys tourists high above the park to Tomorrowland. The view is great, and sometimes the Skyway can even save a little shoe leather. Usually, however, you could arrive in Tomorrowland much faster by walking.

TOURING TIPS   We enjoy this scenic trip in the morning, during the afternoon Character Parade, during an evening Electrical Parade, or just before closing (this ride sometimes opens later and closes earlier than other rides in Fantasyland). In short, before the crowds fill the park, when they are otherwise occupied or when they are on the decline. These times also provide the most dramatic and beautiful vistas.

Peter Pan's Flight

DESCRIPTION AND COMMENTS   Though not considered to be one of the major attractions, Peter Pan's Flight is superbly designed and absolutely delightful with a happy theme, a reunion with some unforgettable Disney characters, beautiful effects, and charming music.

TOURING TIPS   Though not a major feature of the Magic Kingdom, we nevertheless classify it as "not to be missed." Try to ride before 11:30 A.M. or after 5:00 P.M., or during the afternoon Character Parade.

Cinderella's Golden Carousel

DESCRIPTION AND COMMENTS   A merry-go-round to be sure, but certainly one of the most elaborate and beautiful you will ever see, especially when the lights are on.

TOURING TIPS   Unless there are small children in your party we suggest you appreciate this ride from the sidelines. If your children insist on riding, try to get on before 11:30 A.M. or after 5:00 P.M. While nice to look at, the Carousel loads and unloads very slowly.

Mr. Toad's Wild Ride

DESCRIPTION AND COMMENTS   This is an amusement park spook house that does not live up to most visitors' expectations or to the Disney reputation for high quality. The facade is intriguing; the size of the building which houses the attraction suggests an elaborate ride. As it happens, the building is cut in half with the same lackluster ride reproduced in both halves. There is, of course, a separate line for each half.

TOURING TIPS   Skip this ride or let the kids ride if you have some extra time and the lines are short. Also, don't worry that the ride is called "wild"; it's not.

Snow White's Scary Adventures

DESCRIPTION AND COMMENTS   Here you ride in a mining car through a spook house featuring Snow White as she narrowly escapes harm at the hands of the wicked witch. The action and effects are a cut above Mr. Toad's Wild Ride but not as good as Peter Pan's Flight.

TOURING TIPS   This ride is not great, but it is good. Experience it if the lines are not too long or on a second day visit. Ride before noon or after 5:00 P.M. if possible. Also, don't take the "Scary" part too seriously. The witch looks mean but most kids take her in stride.

20,000 Leagues Under the Sea

DESCRIPTION AND COMMENTS   This attraction is based on the Disney movie of the same title. One of several rides that have been successful at both Disneyland (California) and the Magic Kingdom, the ride consists of a submarine voyage which encounters ocean-floor farming, various marine life (robotic), sunken ships, giant squid attacks, and other sights and adventures. An older ride, it struggles to maintain its image along with such marvels as Pirates of the Caribbean or Space Mountain. All things considered, though, it's still a darn nifty experience, and one that we put in our "not to be missed" category.

TOURING TIPS   This is a slow-loading, relatively low-capacity ride. To avoid long lines, ride before 11:00 A.M. or right before the park closes. Note that we do list 20,000 Leagues as a "not to be missed" attraction.

Dumbo, the Flying Elephant

DESCRIPTION AND COMMENTS   A nice, tame, happy children's ride based on the lovable Disney flying elephant, Dumbo. An upgraded rendition of a ride that can be found at state fairs and amusement parks across the country.

TOURING TIPS   This is a slow-loading ride that we recommend you bypass unless you are on a very relaxed touring schedule. If your kids are excited about Dumbo, try to get them on the ride before 11:30 A.M. or just before the park closes.

Mad Tea Party

DESCRIPTION AND COMMENTS   Well done in the Disney style, but still just an amusement-park ride. The Alice in Wonderland Mad Hatter provides the theme and riders whirl around feverishly in big tea cups. A rendition of this ride, sans Disney characters, can be found at every local carnival and fair.

TOURING TIPS   This ride, aside from not being particularly unique, is notoriously slow loading. Skip it on a busy schedule if the kids will let you. Ride in the morning of your second day if your schedule is more relaxed.

Fantasyland Eateries and Shops

DESCRIPTION AND COMMENTS   It's no big secret that we find the food in the Magic Kingdom edible but certainly mediocre. Fantasyland food is no exception. If you prefer atmosphere with your dining, however, you can (with reservations) eat in Cinderella Castle at King Stefan's Banquet Hall. Many of the Magic Kingdom visitors we surveyed wanted to know "What is in the castle?" or "Can we go up into the castle?" Well, Virginia, you can't see the whole thing, but if you eat at King Stefan's you can inspect a fair-sized chunk.

Shops here present more specialty and souvenir shopping opportunities.

TOURING TIPS   To eat at King Stefan's in the castle you must have reservations. Go first thing in the morning and get in line at the door of the restaurant in the interior archway of the castle. We do not recommend a meal at King Stefan's if you are on a tight schedule. If you plan to spend two days in the Magic Kingdom and you are curious about the inside of the castle, you might give it a try on your second day. Don't waste time in the shops unless you have a relaxed schedule or unless shopping is a big priority.

Tomorrowland

Tomorrowland is a futuristic mix of rides and experiences that relate to the technological development of man and what life will be like in the years to come. If this sounds a little bit like the EPCOT Center theme, it's because Tomorrowland was very much a breeding ground for the ideas that resulted in EPCOT Center. Yet Tomorrowland and EPCOT Center are very different. Aside from differences in scale, Tomorrowland is more "just for fun." While EPCOT Center educates in its own delightful style, Tomorrowland allows you to hop in and try the future on for size.

Space Mountain

DESCRIPTION AND COMMENTS   Space Mountain is a roller coaster in the dark. Totally enclosed in a mammoth futuristic structure, the attraction is a marvel of creativity and engineering. The theme of the ride is a spaceflight through the dark recesses of the galaxy. The effects are superb and the ride is the fastest and wildest in the Disney repertoire. As a roller coaster, Space Mountain is a lulu, much zippier than the Big Thunder Mountain ride.

TOURING TIPS   Space Mountain is a "not to be missed" feature (if you can handle a fairly wild roller coaster ride). People who are not timid about going on roller coasters will take Space Mountain in stride. What sets Space Mountain apart is that the cars plummet through the dark with only occasional lighting effects piercing the gloom. Try to ride Space Mountain before 10:30 A.M. or in the hour before the park closes.

Grand Prix Raceway

DESCRIPTION AND COMMENTS   An elaborate miniature raceway with gasoline-powered cars that will travel at speeds of up to seven miles an hour. The raceway design with its sleek cars, racing noises, and Grand Prix billboards is quite alluring. Unfortunately, however, the cars poke along on a track leaving the driver with little to do. Pretty ho hum for most adults and teenagers. Of those children who would enjoy the ride, many are excluded by the requirement that drivers be 4'4" tall.

TOURING TIPS   This ride is appealing to the eye but definitely expendable to the schedule. Try it your second day if the kids are reluctant to omit it. Ride before 11:00 A.M. or after 4:30 P.M.

Skyway to Fantasyland

DESCRIPTION AND COMMENTS   A skylift that will transport you from Tomorrowland to the far corner of Fantasyland near the border it shares with Liberty Square. The view is one of the best in the Magic Kingdom, but walking is usually faster if you just want to get there.

TOURING TIPS   Unless the lines are short, the Skyway will not save you any time as a mode of transportation. As a ride, however, it affords some incredible views. Ride in the morning, during the two hours before the park closes, or during one of the daily parades (this ride sometimes opens later and closes earlier than other rides in Tomorrowland).

StarJets

DESCRIPTION AND COMMENTS   A carnival-type ride involving small rockets which rotate on arms around a central axis.

TOURING TIPS   Slow loading and expendable on any schedule.

WEDway PeopleMover

DESCRIPTION AND COMMENTS   A unique prototype of a linear induction powered system of mass transportation. Tram-like cars take you on a leisurely tour of Tomorrowland, including a peek at the inside of Space Mountain.

TOURING TIPS   A nice, pleasant, relaxing ride where the lines move quickly and are seldom long. A good ride to take during the busier times of the day.

Carousel of Progress

DESCRIPTION AND COMMENTS   This is a warm and nostalgic look at the way technology and electricity have changed the lives of an Audio-Animatronics family over several generations. Though not rating a "not to be missed" review, General Electric's Carousel of Progress is thoroughly delightful. The family depicted is easy to identify with, and a happy, sentimental tune (which you will find yourself humming all day) serves to bridge the gap between generations.

TOURING TIPS   While not on our "not to be missed" list, this attraction is a great favorite of Magic Kingdom repeat visitors. A great favorite of ours as well, it is included on all of our One-Day Touring Plans. Carousel of Progress handles big crowds effectively and is a good choice for touring during the busier times of the day.

If You Had Wings

DESCRIPTION AND COMMENTS   Presented by Eastern Airlines, this ride combines special effects with a travelogue in a whirlwind tour of the globe. Many of the cinematic effects so typical of EPCOT Center were pioneered on this ride. Happy and relaxed with a couple of surprises, the attraction is both fun and worthwhile.

TOURING TIPS   A fast-loading, high-carrying-capacity ride, If You Had Wings is another good choice for touring when the crowd is at its peak. While not awarded "not to be missed" status, the attraction is definitely worth your time.

Circle-Vision 360: American Journeys

DESCRIPTION AND COMMENTS   Here the visitor stands in the center of a huge theater where multiple projectors make an encircling 360° screen come alive. It's another trip around the world, but this time you not only see where you are going, but what's on either side, and what's behind you. The movie, which demonstrates this cinematic marvel, is fast paced, well produced, and very much deserving of your attention. More than a travelogue, *American Journeys* takes you down the awesome rapids of the Colorado River, on a surfing expedition in Hawaii, and in close for a space-shuttle blast-off.

TOURING TIPS   An excellent film and an exciting new motion picture technique make this an attraction you will want to see. The theater has the largest single-room capacity of any theater in the Magic Kingdom, making it a perfect show to see during peak attendance hours.

Mission to Mars

DESCRIPTION AND COMMENTS   Here the visitor takes a simulated space shuttle flight from Earth to Mars. The voyage is both dramatic and educational, with realistic special effects.

TOURING TIPS   A long-enduring Magic Kingdom favorite (formerly Spaceflight to the Moon), this attraction still demands attention. Try to see Mission to Mars before 11:00 A.M. or after 5:00 P.M.

Tomorrowland Eateries and Shops

DESCRIPTION AND COMMENTS   The Tomorrowland Terrace is the largest and most efficient of the Magic Kingdom's numerous fast-food restaurants. This is the one place where you *might* be able to grab a bite during normal meal hours without waiting in line half the day. The food is as elsewhere in the park, edible but undistinguished.

Several shops provide yet additional opportunities for buying souvenirs and curiosities.

TOURING TIPS   The Tomorrowland Terrace may be the least time-consuming eatery in the park for lunch and dinner. If you are in the neighborhood at meal time give it a try.

Forget browsing the shops until your second day unless shopping is your top priority.

Magic Kingdom Ride Information

There are many different types of rides in the Magic Kingdom. Some rides, like Pirates of the Caribbean, are engineered to carry almost 3,500 people every hour. At the other extreme, rides such as Dumbo, the Flying Elephant, can only accommodate around 300 persons in an hour. Most rides fall somewhere in between. Lots of factors figure into how long you will have to wait to experience a particular ride: the popularity of the ride, how it loads and unloads, how many persons can ride at one time, how many units (cars, rockets, boats, flying elephants, Skyway gondolas, etc.) of those available are in service at a given time, and how many staff personnel are available to operate the ride. Let's take them one by one:

1. *How popular is the ride?*

Newer rides like Big Thunder Mountain Railroad attract a lot of people, as do longtime favorites such as 20,000 Leagues Under the Sea. If you know a ride is popular, you need to learn a little more about how it operates to determine when might be the best time to ride. But a ride need not be especially popular to form long lines; the lines can be the result of less than desirable traffic engineering (i.e., it takes so long to load and unload that a line builds up anyway). This is the situation at the Mad Tea Party, Dumbo, the Flying Elephant, and Cinderella's Golden Carousel. For instance, only a small percentage of the visitors (mostly children) to the Magic Kingdom ride Dumbo, but because it takes so long to load and unload this comparatively less popular ride, long waiting lines form.

2. *How does the ride load and unload?*

Some rides never stop. They are like a circular conveyor belt that goes around and around. We call these "continuous loaders." The Haunted Mansion is a continuous loader, and so are If You Had Wings and Peter Pan's Flight. Loading is continuous. The more cars or pirate ships or whatever are on the conveyor, the more people can be moved through in an hour. The Haunted Mansion and If You Had Wings have lots of cars on the conveyor belt and consequently can move more than 2,500 people an hour. Peter Pan's Flight has fewer cars (or pirate ships in this case) and can only handle about 1,100 people each hour.

Still other rides are "interval loaders." This means that cars are unloaded, loaded, and dispatched at certain set intervals (sometimes controlled manually and sometimes by a computer). Space Mountain is an interval loader. It has two separate tracks (in other words the ride has been duplicated in the same facility). Each track can run up to fourteen space capsules, released at thirty-six-second, twenty-six-second, or twenty-one-second intervals (the bigger the crowd, the shorter the interval). In one kind of interval loader, like Space Mountain, empty cars (space capsules) are returned to the starting point empty where they line up waiting to be reloaded. In a second type of interval loader, one group of riders enters the vehicle while the last group of riders depart. We call these "in and out" interval loaders. It's a Small World is a good example of an in and out interval loader. As a boat pulls up to the dock, those who have just completed their ride exit to the left. At almost the same time, those waiting to ride enter the boat from the right. The boat is released to the dispatch point a few yards down the line where it is launched according to whatever second interval is being used. Interval loaders of both types can be very efficient at moving people if (1) the release (launch) interval is relatively short; and (2) the ride can accommodate a large number of vehicles in the system at one time. Since many boats can be floating through Pirates of the Caribbean at a given time, and since the release interval is short, almost 3,500 people an hour can see this attraction. 20,000 Leagues Under the Sea is an in and out interval loader, but can only run a maximum of nine submarines at a time. Thus 20,000 Leagues can only handle up to 1,800 people an hour.

A third group of rides are "cycle rides." Another name for these same rides is "stop and go" rides. Here those waiting to ride exchange places with those who have just ridden. The main difference between in and out interval rides and cycle rides is that with a cycle ride the whole system shuts down when loading and unloading is in progress. While one boat is loading and unloading in It's a Small World many other boats are advancing through the ride. But when Dumbo, the Flying Elephant, touches down, the whole ride is at a standstill until the next flight is launched. Likewise, with Cinderella's Golden Carousel, all riders dismount and the Carousel stands stationary until the next group is mounted and ready to ride. In discussing a cycle ride, the amount of time the ride is in motion is called "ride time." The amount of time that the ride is idle while loading and unloading is called "load time." Load time added to ride time equals "cycle time," or the time expended from the start of one run of the ride until the start of the succeeding run. Cycle rides are the least efficient of all Magic Kingdom rides in terms of traffic engineering.

3. *How many persons can ride at one time?*

This figure is defined in terms of "per ride capacity" or "system capacity." Either way the figures allude to the number of people who can be riding at the same time. Our discussion above illustrates that the greater the carrying capacity of a ride (all other things being equal) the more visitors it can accommodate in an hour.

4. *How many "units" are in service at a given time?*

A "unit" is simply our term for the vehicle you sit in during your ride. At the Mad Tea Party the unit is a tea cup, at 20,000 Leagues it's a submarine, and at the Grand Prix Raceway it's a race car. On some rides (mostly cycle rides), the number of units in operation at a given time is fixed. Thus, there are always ten flying elephant units operating on the Dumbo ride, ninety horses on Cinderella's Golden Carousel, and so on. What this fixed number of units means to you is that there is no way to increase the carrying capacity of the ride by adding more units. On a busy day, therefore, the only way to carry more people each hour on a fixed unit cycle ride is to shorten the loading time (which, as we will discuss next, is sometimes impossible) or by decreasing the riding time, the actual time the ride is in motion. The bottom line on a busy day for a cycle ride is that you will wait longer and be rewarded for your wait with a shorter ride. This is why we try to steer you clear of the cycle rides unless you are willing to ride them early in the morning or late at night. The following are cycle rides:

Fantasyland:	Dumbo, the Flying Elephant
	Cinderella's Golden Carousel
	Mad Tea Party
Tomorrowland:	StarJets

Other rides in the Magic Kingdom can increase their carrying capacity by adding additional units to the system as the crowds build. Big

Thunder Mountain is a good example. If attendance is very light, Big Thunder can start the day by running one of their five available mine trains on one out of two available tracks. If lines start to build the other track can be opened and more mine trains placed into operation. At full capacity a total of five trains on two tracks can carry about 2,400 persons an hour. Likewise Pirates of the Caribbean can increase its capacity by adding more boats, and Snow White's Scary Adventures by adding more mine cars. Sometimes a long line will disappear almost instantly when new units are brought on line. When an interval-loading ride places more units into operation, it usually shortens the dispatch interval, so more units are being dispatched more often.

5. *How many staff personnel are available to operate the ride?*

Allocation of additional staff to a given ride can allow extra units to be placed in operation, or additional loading areas or holding areas to be opened. Pirates of the Caribbean and It's a Small World can run two separate waiting lines and loading zones. The Haunted Mansion has a one-and-a-half-minute preshow which is staged in a "stretch room." On busy days a second stretch room can be activated, thus permitting a more continuous flow of visitors to the actual loading area. Additional staff make a world of difference in some cycle rides. Often, one attendant will operate the Mad Tea Party. This single person must clear the visitors from the ride just completed, admit and seat visitors for the upcoming ride, check that all tea cups are properly secured (which entails an inspection of each tea cup), return to the control panel, issue instructions to the riders, and finally, activate the ride (whew!). A second attendant allows for the division of these responsibilities and has the effect of cutting loading time by 25 to 50 percent.

By knowing the way a ride loads, its approximate hourly capacity, and its relative popularity, we can anticipate which rides are likely to develop long lines, and more importantly, how long we will have to wait to ride. Following is a summary of the important technical information for each ride.

— *Adventureland* —

Jungle Cruise

When to Ride: Before 10:30 A.M. or one hour before closing
Duration of Ride: Almost 9 minutes

Jungle Cruise (continued)

Average Wait in Line per 100 People Ahead of You: 3½ minutes
Assumes: 10 or more boats operating
Loading Method: Interval
Loading Speed: Slow
System Capacity: Approximately 1,700 persons per hour

Swiss Family Island Treehouse

When to Visit: Before noon or after 5 P.M.
Duration of Visit: 10–15 minutes (actually a walk-through exhibit)
Average Wait in Line per 100 People Ahead of You: 7½ minutes
Assumes: Normal, continuous movement through exhibit
Loading Method: Walk-through exhibit; does not load
Loading Speed: NA
System Capacity: Approximately 800 persons per hour

Pirates of the Caribbean

When to Ride: Between 11:30 A.M. and 4:30 P.M.
Duration of Ride: 7½ minutes
Average Wait in Line per 100 People Ahead of You: 1½ minutes
Assumes: Both waiting lines operating
Loading Method: Interval
Loading Speed: Fast
System Capacity: Approximately 3,500 persons per hour

—— *Frontierland* ——

Big Thunder Mountain Railroad

When to Ride: Before 11:00 A.M. or after 5:30 P.M.
Duration of Ride: Almost 3½ minutes
Average Wait in Line per 100 People Ahead of You: 2½ minutes
Assumes: Both tracks running with 5 trains in operation
Loading Method: Interval

Loading Speed: Moderate

System Capacity: 2,400 persons per hour

Tom Sawyer Island Rafts

When to Ride: Before noon or after 5:00 P.M.

Duration of Ride: $1\frac{1}{2}$ minutes (one way)

Average Wait in Line per 100 People Ahead of You: 6 minutes

Assumes: 2 rafts operating

Loading Method: Cycle

Loading Speed: Slow

System Capacity: Approximately 1,000 persons each way per hour

Davy Crockett's Explorer Canoes

When to Ride: Before noon or after 5 P.M.

Duration of Ride: 10–15 minutes depending on how hard you paddle

Average Wait in Line per 100 People Ahead of You: 28 minutes

Assumes: 3 canoes operating

Loading Method: Interval

Loading Speed: Slow

System Capacity: Approximately 216 persons per hour

—— *Liberty Square* ——

Liberty Square Riverboat

When to Ride: Between 11 A.M. and 5 P.M.

Duration of Ride: About 16 minutes

Average Wait in Line per 100 People Ahead of You: People waiting
rarely exceed boat capacity (450); the maximum wait if you just
missed the boat would be 24 minutes

Assumes: 1 riverboat running

Loading Method: Cycle

Loading Speed: Slow

System Capacity: Approximately 1,350 persons every hour and 15
minutes

Mike Fink Keelboats

When to Ride: Before 11:30 A.M. or after 5 P.M.
Duration of Ride: 9½ minutes
Average Wait in Line per 100 People Ahead of You: 15 minutes
Assumes: 2 keelboats operating
Loading Method: Interval
Loading Speed: Slow
System Capacity: 400 persons per hour

Haunted Mansion

When to Ride: Before noon or after 2:30 P.M.
Duration of Ride: 1½-minute preshow, 7-minute ride
Average Wait in Line per 100 People Ahead of You: 2½ minutes
Assumes: Both "stretch rooms" operating
Loading Method: Continuous
Loading Speed: Fast
System Capacity: Approximately 2,600 persons per hour

— Fantasyland —

Skyway to Tomorrowland

When to Ride: Before noon and during special events
Duration of Ride: 5 minutes (one way)
Average Wait in Line per 100 People Ahead of You: 10 minutes
Assumes: 45 or more cars in operation
Loading Method: Interval
Loading Speed: Moderate to slow
System Capacity: Approximately 600 persons per hour from the
    Fantasyland terminus

It's a Small World

When to Ride: Between 11:00 A.M. and 5 P.M.
Duration of Ride: 10½ minutes
Average Wait in Line per 100 People Ahead of You: 1¾ minutes

Assumes: 30 or more boats operating
Loading Method: Interval
Loading Speed: Fast
System Capacity: Approximately 3,500 persons per hour

Peter Pan's Flight

When to Ride: Before 11:30 A.M. or after 5 P.M.
Duration of Ride: A little over 3 minutes
Average Wait in Line per 100 People Ahead of You: 5½ minutes
Assumes: Normal operation
Loading Method: Continuous
Loading Speed: Moderate
System Capacity: Approximately 1,100 persons per hour

Cinderella's Golden Carousel

When to Ride: Before 11 A.M. or after 5 P.M.
Duration of Ride: 1¾–2 minutes
Average Wait in Line per 100 People Ahead of You: 5 minutes
Assumes: Normal staffing
Loading Method: Cycle
Loading Speed: Slow
System Capacity: Approximately 1,100 persons per hour

Dumbo, the Flying Elephant

When to Ride: Before 11 A.M. or after 5 P.M.
Duration of Ride: 1½ minutes
Average Wait in Line per 100 People Ahead of You: 20 minutes
Assumes: Normal Staffing
Loading Method: Cycle
Loading Speed: Slow
System Capacity: Approximately 300 persons per hour

Snow White's Scary Adventures

When to Ride: Before 11:30 A.M. or after 5 P.M.
Duration of Ride: Almost 2½ minutes

Snow White's Scary Adventures (continued)

Average Wait in Line per 100 People Ahead of You: $6\frac{1}{4}$ minutes
Assumes: Normal operation
Loading Method: Interval
Loading Speed: Moderate
System Capacity: Approximately 960 persons per hour

Mr. Toad's Wild Ride

When to Ride: Before noon or after 5 P.M.
Duration of Ride: $2\frac{1}{4}$ minutes
Average Wait in Line per 100 People Ahead of You: $5\frac{1}{2}$ minutes
Assumes: Both tracks operating
Loading Method: Interval
Loading Speed: Moderate
System Capacity: Approximately 1,100 persons per hour

20,000 Leagues Under the Sea

When to Ride: Before 10:30 A.M.
Duration of Ride: $8\frac{1}{2}$ minutes
Average Wait in Line per 100 People Ahead of You: $3\frac{1}{2}$ minutes
Assumes: 9 submarines operating
Loading Method: Interval
Loading Speed: Moderate to slow
System Capacity: Approximately 1,800 persons per hour

Mad Tea Party

When to Ride: Before 11:30 A.M. or after 5 P.M.
Duration of Ride: $1\frac{1}{2}$ minutes
Average Wait in Line per 100 People Ahead of You: $7\frac{1}{2}$ minutes
Assumes: Normal staffing
Loading Method: Cycle
Loading Speed: Slow
System Capacity: Approximately 800 persons per hour

— *Tomorrowland* —

Grand Prix Raceway

When to Ride: Before 11:00 A.M. or after 5 P.M.
Duration of Ride: Approximately 4¼ minutes
Average Wait in Line per 100 People Ahead of You: 4½ minutes
Assumes: 285-car turnover every 20 minutes
Loading Method: Interval
Loading Speed: Moderate
System Capacity: Approximately 1,200 persons per hour

Space Mountain

When to Ride: Before 10:30 A.M. or in the hour before the park closes
Duration of Ride: About 3 minutes
Average Wait in Line per 100 People Ahead of You: 2¾ minutes
Assumes: 2 tracks, 14 capsules per track, 21-second dispatch interval
Loading Method: Interval
Loading Speed: Moderate
System Capacity: Approximately 2,200 persons per hour

Skyway to Fantasyland

When to Ride: Before noon and during special events
Duration of Ride: 5 minutes (one way)
Average Wait in Line per 100 People Ahead of You: 10 minutes
Assumes: 45 or more cars in operation
Loading Method: Interval
Loading Speed: Moderate to slow
System Capacity: Approximately 600 persons per hour from the
   Tomorrowland terminus

StarJets

When to Ride: Before 11 A.M. or after 5 P.M.
Duration of Ride: About 1½ minutes
Average Wait in Line per 100 People Ahead of You: 13½ minutes

StarJets (*continued*)

Assumes: Normal staffing
Loading Method: Cycle
Loading Speed: Slow
System Capacity: Approximately 440 persons per hour

WEDway PeopleMover

When to Ride: Between 11:30 A.M. and 4:30 P.M.
Duration of Ride: About 10 minutes
Average Wait in Line per 100 People Ahead of You: 1½ minutes
Assumes: 39 trains operating
Loading Method: Continuous
Loading Speed: Fast
System Capacity: Approximately 4,500 persons per hour

If You Had Wings

When to Ride: Between 11:30 A.M. and 4:30 P.M.
Duration of Ride: Almost 4½ minutes
Average Wait in Line per 100 People Ahead of You: 2¼ minutes
Assumes: Normal operation
Loading Method: Continuous
Loading Speed: Fast
System Capacity: Approximately 2,700 persons per hour

Magic Kingdom
Theater Information

—— Cutting Down Your Time in Line
by Understanding the Shows ——

Many of the featured attractions in the Magic Kingdom are theater presentations. While not as complex from a traffic engineering viewpoint as rides, a little enlightenment concerning their operation may save some touring time.

Most of the theater attractions in the Magic Kingdom operate in three distinct phases:

1. There are the visitors who are in the theater viewing the presentation.

2. There are the visitors who have passed through the turnstile into a holding area or waiting lobby. These people will be admitted to the theater as soon as the current presentation is concluded. Several attractions offer a preshow in their waiting lobby to entertain the crowd until they are admitted to the main show. Among these are the *Tropical Serenade (Enchanted Tiki Birds)*, and the Mission to Mars.

3. There is the outside line. Visitors waiting here will enter the waiting lobby when there is room, and then be moved into the theater when the audience turns over (is exchanged) between shows.

The theater capacity and the popularity of the presentation, along with the level of attendance in the park, determine how long the lines will be at a given theater attraction. Following is a summary of specific information concerning each theater attraction that should help you plan your visit.

—— How to Deal with Obnoxious People ——

At every theater presentation at both the Magic Kingdom and EPCOT Center, visitors in the preshow area elbow, nudge, and crowd one another in order to make sure that they are admitted to the performance. Not necessary—if you are admitted through the turnstile into the preshow area a seat has automatically been allocated for you in the theater. When it is time to proceed into the theater don't rush; just relax and let other people jam the doorways. When the congestion has been relieved simply stroll in and take a seat.

Attendants at many theaters will instruct you to enter a row of seats and move completely to the far side, filling every seat so that each row can be completely filled. And invariably some inconsiderate, thick-skulled yahoo will plop down right in the middle of the row, stopping traffic or forcing other visitors to climb over him. Take our word for it—there is no such thing as a bad seat. All of the Disney theaters have been designed to provide a near perfect view from every seat in the house. Our recommendation is to follow instructions and move to the far end of the row, and if you encounter some dummy blocking the middle of the row, have every person in your party step very hard on his toes as you move past him.

The Disney people also ask that visitors not use flash photography in the theaters (the theaters are too dark for the pictures to turn out, *plus* the flash is disruptive to other viewers). Needless to say, this admonition is routinely ignored. Flashers are more difficult to deal with than row-blockers. You can threaten to turn the offenders over to Disney Security, or better yet, simply hold your hand over the lens (you have to be quick) when they raise their cameras.

—— *Adventureland* ——

Tropical Serenade (Enchanted Tiki Birds)

When to Go: Before noon and after 2 P.M.
Duration of Presentation: 15 minutes
Preshow Entertainment: 2 minutes
Theater Capacity per Performance: Approximately 330 persons
Theater Capacity: Approximately 1,000 persons per hour

—— *Frontierland* ——

Country Bear Jamboree

When to Go: Before noon and during the two hours before closing
Duration of Presentation: About 15 minutes

Preshow Entertainment: None

Theater Capacity per Performance: Approximately 350 persons

Theater Capacity: Approximately 1,400 persons per hour

NOTE: This is a very popular attraction with a comparatively small seating capacity. An average waiting time on a busy day between the hours of noon and 5:30 P.M. would be from 30 to 50 minutes.

The Diamond Horseshoe Revue (*Reservation only*)

When to Go: As per your reservation

Duration of Presentation: 30 minutes

Preshow Entertainment: 5 minutes

Theater Capacity per Performance: 260–300 depending on party sizes

Theater Capacity: NA

—— *Liberty Square* ——

Hall of Presidents

When to Go: Before noon or after 4 P.M.

Duration of Presentation: A little over 22 minutes

Preshow Entertainment: None

Theater Capacity per Performance: Approximately 750 persons

Theater Capacity: Approximately 2,200 persons every hour and 10 minutes

NOTE: Lines for this attraction LOOK awesome but are usually swallowed up as the theater turns over. It is rare to wait more than 40 minutes at the Hall of Presidents.

—— *Fantasyland* ——

Fantasy Follies

When to Go: At any scheduled performance time

Duration of Presentation: Varies as shows change, but usually about 20–23 minutes

Preshow Entertainment: None

Fantasy Follies (continued)

Theater Capacity per Performance: Approximately 450 persons
Theater Capacity: NA

NOTE: This show runs according to a performance schedule posted in front of the Fantasy Faire Theater (i.e., performances are not continuous). Usually there is no problem gaining admittance, even during the busier times of day.

—— Tomorrowland ——

Carousel of Progress

When to Go: Between 11:30 A.M. and 4 P.M.
Duration of Presentation: 18 minutes
Preshow Entertainment: None
Theater Capacity per Performance: Approximately 1,440 persons
Theater Capacity: Approximately 4,000 persons per hour

American Journeys

When to Go: Between 11:30 A.M. and 4 P.M.
Duration of Presentation: Almost 21 minutes
Preshow Entertainment: Laser and slide show
Theater Capacity per Performance: Approximately 1,200 persons
Theater Capacity: Approximately 3,600 persons in a little over an hour

Mission to Mars

When to Go: Before 11 A.M. or after 4:30 P.M.
Duration of Presentation: 12 minutes
Preshow Entertainment: 6 minutes
Theater Capacity per Performance: Two theaters with a capacity of 120 persons each
Theater Capacity: Approximately 1,100 persons per hour

— *Main Street, U.S.A.* —

Walt Disney Story

When to Go: Between 11 A.M. and 4:30 P.M.

Duration of Presentation: 23 minutes

Preshow Entertainment: None

Theater Capacity per Performance: Two theaters each having a capacity of 260 persons

Theater Capacity: Approximately 1,400 persons per hour

Main Street Cinema (*Continuous-run vintage movies and cartoons*)

When to Go: Between 10 A.M. and one and one-half hours before the park closes

Duration of Presentation: Continuous

Preshow Entertainment: None

Theater Capacity per Performance: Approximately 60 persons

Theater Capacity: NA

Live Entertainment in
the Magic Kingdom

Live entertainment in the form of bands, Disney character appearances, parades, singing and dancing, and ceremonies further enliven and add color to the Magic Kingdom on a daily basis. For specific information about what's going on the day you visit, stop by City Hall as you enter the park. Be forewarned, however, that if you are on a tight schedule, it is impossible to see both the Magic Kingdom's featured attractions **and** take in the numerous and varied live performances offered. In our One-Day Touring Plans we exclude the live performances (except the *Fantasy Follies*) in favor of seeing as much of the park as time permits. This is a considered, tactical decision based on the fact that some of the parades and other performances siphon crowds away from the more popular rides, thus shortening waiting lines.

But the color and pageantry of live happenings around the park are an integral part of the Magic Kingdom entertainment mix and a persuasive argument for second-day touring. The following is an incomplete list and description of those performances and events that are scheduled with some regularity and for which no reservations are required.

Dapper Dans	A barbershop quartet which entertains at various times along Main Street.
Kids of the Kingdom	A youthful song and dance group which performs popular music daily in the Castle Forecourt. Disney characters usually join in the fun.
Flag Retreat	Daily at 5:15 P.M. at Liberty Square, a small band and honor guard lower the flag and release a flock of white homing pigeons.
Main Street Parade	A parade down Main Street and around the central hub featuring marching bands, old-time vehicles, floats, and the Disney characters. Check with City Hall for the parade schedule.

The Great Main Street Electrical Parade	An elaborated version of the Main Street Parade with thirty floats, more than one hundred performers, and "a million twinkling lights," according to Disney spokesmen. The Electrical Parade is performed twice on holidays and on days when the park is open until midnight, usually at 9:00 P.M. and 11:00 P.M.
Bay Lake and Seven Seas Lagoon Floating Electrical Pageant	This is one of our favorites of all the Disney extras, but you have to exit the Magic Kingdom to see it. The Floating Electrical Pageant is a stunning electric light show afloat on small barges and set to nifty electronic music. The Pageant is performed at nightfall on the Seven Seas Lagoon and on Bay Lake. Exit the Magic Kingdom and take the monorail to the Contemporary Resort Hotel or to the Polynesian Village. Proceed to get yourself a drink and have a seat at the waterfront; the show will begin shortly.
Fantasy in the Sky	A stellar fireworks display unleashed after dark on those nights the park is open until midnight.
Tomorrowland Terrace Stage	The stage at Tomorrowland Terrace is the site of daily concerts, usually featuring rock, pop, and electronic music.
Disney Character Show (*Fantasy Follies*)	Song and dance stage shows featuring the Disney characters performed according to a posted schedule at the Fantasy Faire Theater (formerly the *Mickey Mouse Review*). The theater is situated in Fantasyland opposite Cinderella's Golden Carousel.
Magic Kingdom Bands	Various banjo, dixieland, steel drum, marching, and fife and drum bands roam the Magic Kingdom daily.
Walt Disney Character Appearances	Walt Disney characters appear at random throughout the Magic Kingdom but seemingly with more frequency in Fantasyland and on Main Street.

Eating in the Magic Kingdom

The Magic Kingdom is a wonder and a marvel, a testimony to the creative genius of man. But for all of the beauty, imagination, and wholesomeness of this incredible place, it is virtually impossible to obtain a decent meal. Simply put, what is available is food for the masses—bland, undistinguished, bulk. Logistically we are sympathetic; it is overwhelming to contemplate preparing and serving 100,000 or so meals each day. But our understanding, unfortunately, does not make the food any more palatable. Do not misunderstand, the food at the Magic Kingdom is not awful. It is merely mediocre in a place that has set the standard in virtually every other area for quality in tourism and entertainment. Given the challenge of feeding so many people each day, we might be more accepting of the benign fare if (1) we didn't believe the Disney people could do better, and if (2) obtaining food didn't require such an investment of time and effort. The variety found on the numerous menus indicates that somebody once had the right idea. Unfortunately, something was lost in the preparation and what looks good on the printed menu loses its appeal when it appears on your plate.

— Alternatives and Suggestions for Eating in the Magic Kingdom —

Remember, this discussion is about the Magic Kingdom. EPCOT Center is a whole new game and is treated separately under a similar heading on page 142.

1. Eat a good breakfast before arriving at the Magic Kingdom. You do not want to waste touring time eating breakfast at the park. Besides, there are some truly outstanding breakfast specials at restaurants outside of Walt Disney World.

2. Having eaten a good breakfast, keep your tummy happy as you tour by purchasing snacks from the many vendors stationed through-

out the Magic Kingdom (or expressed differently—avoid restaurants!). This is especially important if you have a tight schedule; you cannot afford to spend a lot of time waiting in line for food.

3. If you are on a tight schedule and the park closes early, stay until closing and eat dinner outside of Walt Disney World before returning to your hotel. If the Magic Kingdom stays open late, eat an early dinner at about 4 P.M. or 4:30 P.M. in the Magic Kingdom eatery of your choice. You should have missed the last wave of lunch diners and sneaked in just ahead of the dinner crowd.

4. If you are on a fairly relaxed schedule with more than one day allocated for touring the Magic Kingdom, try leaving the park for lunch at one of the many restaurants outside of Walt Disney World. The coming and going isn't nearly as time consuming as it appears, and you will probably be able to get a better meal, with faster service, in a more relaxed atmosphere, at a cheaper price.

5. Take the monorail to one of the Theme Resort Hotels for lunch. The trip over and back takes very little time, and because most guests have left the hotels for the parks, the Theme Resort restaurants are often slack. The food is not much better than in the Magic Kingdom, but the service is faster, the atmosphere more relaxed, and beer, wine, and mixed drinks are available. Of the two Theme Resorts connected directly to the Magic Kingdom by monorail, we vastly prefer the fare of the Contemporary Resort Hotel. A good restaurant for lunch is the Terrace Buffeteria on the Grand Canyon Concourse. We have tried every eating place in the Polynesian Village and have been consistently disappointed.

6. If you are bound and determined to eat in the Magic Kingdom during the midday rush (11 A.M.–2 P.M.) or during the evening rush (5 P.M.–8 P.M.), try the Tomorrowland Terrace, the park's largest eating establishment. The food is no better than elsewhere, but the service and crowd management are more efficient.

7. Many of the Magic Kingdom restaurants serve a cold sandwich of one sort or another. It is possible to buy a cold lunch (except for the drinks) before 11 A.M. and then carry your food until you are ready to eat. We met a family which does this routinely, with Mom always remembering to bring several small plastic bags in which to pack the food. Drinks are purchased at an appropriate time from any convenient drink vendor.

8. Most fast-food eateries in the Magic Kingdom have more than one service window. Regardless of time of day, check out the lines at *all* of the windows before queuing. Sometimes a manned, but out of the way, window will have a much shorter line or no line at all.

9. Don't expect quantum leaps in food quality if you eat in a sit-down, waitress-service restaurant. The atmosphere will be nicer, the prices higher, and the names of the entrees fancier, but the food will still be lackluster.

10. Restaurants which accept reservations for lunch and/or dinner fill their respective meal seatings quickly. To obtain reservations you must hot-foot it over to the restaurant in question (King Stefan's Banquet Hall, the Diamond Horseshoe Saloon, etc.) as soon as you enter the park and blow your most effective touring time waiting in line to make your meal reservation. Often you are asked to return well in advance of your seating time, and even then, on many occasions, you will have to wait well past your scheduled time for your table.

11. For your general information, the Disney people have a park rule against bringing in your own food and drink. We interviewed one woman who, ignoring the rule, brought a huge picnic lunch for her family of five packed into a large diaper/baby paraphernalia bag. Upon entering the park she secured the bag in a locker under the Main Street Station, to be retrieved later when the family was hungry. A Texas family returned to their camper/truck in the parking lot for lunch where they had a cooler, lawn chairs, and plenty of food a la the college football tailgating tradition.

Shopping in the Magic Kingdom

Shops in the Magic Kingdom add realism and atmosphere to the various theme settings and make available an extensive inventory of souvenirs, clothing, novelties, decorator items, and more. Much of the merchandise displayed (with the exception of Disney trademark souvenir items) is available back home and elsewhere at a lower price. In our opinion, shopping is not one of the main reasons for visiting the Magic Kingdom. We recommend bypassing the shops on a one-day visit. If you have two or more days to spend in the Magic Kingdom, browse the shops during the early afternoon when many of the attractions are crowded. Remember that Main Street, with its multitude of shops, opens one hour earlier and closes one hour later than the rest of the park. Lockers in the Main Street Train Station allow you to stash your purchases safely as opposed to dragging them around the park with you.

Magic Kingdom
One-Day Touring Plans

The Magic Kingdom One-Day Touring Plans are field-tested, step-by-step plans for seeing as much as possible in one day with a minimum of time wasted standing in line. They are designed to assist you in avoiding crowds and bottlenecks on days of moderate to heavy attendance. On days of lighter attendance (see Selecting the Time of Year for Your Visit, page 18), the plans will still save you time, but will not be as critical to successful touring as on busier days. Do not be concerned that other people will be following the same touring strategy, thus rendering it useless. Fewer than 1 of every 300 people in the park will have been exposed to this information.

On days of moderate to heavy attendance follow the One-Day Touring Plan exactly, deviating only:

1. When you do not wish to experience an attraction called for on the Touring Plan. For instance, the Touring Plan may indicate that you go next to Tomorrowland and ride Space Mountain, a roller coaster ride. If you do not enjoy roller coasters, simply skip this step of the plan and proceed to the next step.

2. When you encounter a very long line at an attraction called for by the Touring Plan. Crowds ebb and flow at the Magic Kingdom, and by chance an unusually large line may have gathered at an attraction to which you are directed. For example, upon arrival at the Haunted Mansion, you find the waiting lines to be extremely long. It is possible that this is a temporary situation occasioned by several hundred people arriving en masse from a recently concluded performance of the nearby Hall of Presidents. If this is the case, simply skip the Haunted Mansion and move to the next step, returning later in the day to try the Haunted Mansion once again.

Three outline versions of the One-Day Touring Plan follow this section; each is tailored for groups with different needs.

—— *Traffic Patterns in the Magic Kingdom* ——

When we began our research on the Magic Kingdom we were very interested in traffic patterns throughout the park, specifically:

1. *Which sections of the park and what attractions do visitors head for when they first arrive?* When visitors are admitted to the various lands the flow of people to Tomorrowland, Fantasyland, and Adventureland is almost equal. The flow initially to Liberty Square and to Frontierland is slightly less. In our research we tested the assertion, often heard, that most people turn right into Tomorrowland and tour the Magic Kingdom in an orderly counterclockwise fashion. We found it without basis. As the park fills visitors appear to head for specific favored attractions which they wish to ride before the lines get long. This more than any other factor determines traffic patterns in the mornings, and accounts for a relatively equal distribution of visitors throughout the Magic Kingdom. Attractions which receive considerable patronage in the early morning are:

Tomorrowland:	Space Mountain
Frontierland:	*The Diamond Horseshoe Revue*
	Big Thunder Mountain Railroad
Fantasyland:	20,000 Leagues Under the Sea
Adventureland:	Jungle Cruise

2. *How long does it take for the park to reach peak capacity for a given day? How are the visitors dispersed throughout the park?* Lines sampled reached their longest length between noon and 2 P.M., indicating more arrivals than park departures into the early afternoon. For general touring purposes, most attractions developed substantial lines between 10:30 A.M. and 11:30 A.M. Through the early hours of the morning and the early hours of the afternoon attendance was fairly equally distributed through all of the lands. In late afternoon, however, we noted a concentration of visitors in Fantasyland, Liberty Square, and Frontierland, with a slight decrease of visitors in Adventureland, and a marked decrease of visitors in Tomorrowland. This pattern did not occur consistently day to day, but did happen often enough for us to suggest Tomorrowland as the least crowded land for late afternoon touring.

3. *How do most visitors go about touring the park? Is there a difference in the touring behavior of first-time visitors versus repeat visitors?* Many first time visitors accompany friends or relatives who are familiar with the Magic Kingdom and guide their tour. These tours sometimes do and sometimes do not proceed in an orderly touring sequence. First-time visitors without personal touring guides tend to be more orderly in their touring. Many first-time visitors, however, are drawn to Cinderella Castle upon entering the park and thus commence their rotation from Fantasyland. Repeat visitors usually proceed directly to their favorite attractions.

4. *What effect do special events, such as the daily Main Street Parade, have on traffic patterns?* Special events such as the Main Street Parade do pull substantial numbers of visitors from the ride lines, but the key to the length of the lines remains the number of people in the park.

5. *What are the traffic patterns near to and at closing time?* On our sample days, in season and out of season, park departures outnumbered arrivals beginning mid-afternoon. A substantial number of visitors departed during the late afternoon as the dinner hour approached. When the park closed early there were steady departures during the two hours preceding closing time, with a huge mass exodus of remaining visitors at closing time. When the park closed late, departures were distributed throughout the evening hours, increasing as closing time approached, with a huge throng still on hand to depart at closing time. The balloon effect of mass departures at closing time primarily impacts on conditions on Main Street and at the monorail and ferry embarkation points due to the relatively sudden consolidation of the crowds when the other five lands close. In the other five lands just prior to closing, touring conditions are normally uncrowded.

— *Magic Kingdom One-Day Touring Plan, for Adults* —

FOR: **Adults without small children.**

ASSUMES: Willingness to experience all major rides (including roller coasters) and shows.

DIRECTION	EXPLANATION
1. Arrive at the main parking lot one hour and fifteen minutes before the park's stated opening time.	This will allow you to be one of the first visitors in the park which will permit you to board many popular rides without long waits in line.
2. Take the monorail to the Magic Kingdom from the Transportation and Ticket Center.	Your choice of transportation to the Magic Kingdom consists of a ferryboat or the monorail. Lines are longer for the monorail, but even so you will usually arrive at the Magic Kingdom ahead of the boat.
3. Do not stop on Main Street, except to pick up a schedule of the day's live entertainment and special events at City Hall. Proceed to the end of Main Street and wait to be admitted to the rest of the park.	Main Street opens before the rest of the Magic Kingdom and consists primarily of shops and eateries. Since your objective is to beat the crowds to the potential bottlenecks in the other areas of the park, you will postpone seeing Main Street until later when traffic has dispersed and rides in other sections of the park have become crowded. Now you want to position yourself at the central hub so that you will be one of the first to arrive at the first ride on the Touring Plan.

DIRECTION	EXPLANATION
4. Turn left into Adventureland and ride the Jungle Cruise.	This is a major ride and a very slow loader. If you do not ride early in the morning you will have a long wait later.
5. Go next to Frontierland and ride the Big Thunder Mountain Railroad.	A newer and very popular ride that loads at moderate speed; if you do not ride early in the morning you will have a long wait later.
6. Go next to Fantasyland and ride 20,000 Leagues Under the Sea.	A popular ride but very slow loading. If you do not ride early in the morning you will have a long wait later.
7. While in Fantasyland, ride Snow White's Scary Adventures.	This is a relatively slow-loading ride which will develop long lines later in the day.
8. While in Fantasyland, ride Peter Pan's Flight.	Another relatively slow-loading ride which will develop long lines later in the day.

NOTE: With Step 9 the Touring Plan shifts from the slower-loading and/ or low-capacity rides and shows (which need to be visited earlier in the day before the park fills) to rides and shows which are engineered to handle large crowds effectively even at peak attendance.

9. Proceed to Liberty Square and see the Haunted Mansion.	The Haunted Mansion is a continuous-load ride with above average capability to move crowds.
10. Go next to the Hall of Presidents in Liberty Square and ask when the next show is scheduled to begin. If a show is scheduled within fifteen minutes, stay and see it. If you would have to wait longer than fifteen minutes, go on to Step 11.	The number of people waiting for this attraction usually does not exceed its capacity (i.e., everyone waiting in line will generally be accommodated at the next Hall of Presidents show). Note that when visitors are admitted to the Hall of Presidents they are admitted only

DIRECTION	EXPLANATION
	to a lobby where they wait up to twenty-three minutes to be admitted to the show. The touring strategy here is to be admitted as close to showtime as possible without being held over for the next show.
11. Proceed to Frontierland and see the *Country Bear Jamboree.*	You will have a wait here but it should not be a bad one. Stick it out, the lines will get longer later in the day.

NOTE: This is about as far as you can go before the crowds catch up with you on a busy day, but you will have experienced eight of the more popular rides and shows before the park fills up. On slower days you might be able to squeeze in one more major ride before the crunch hits. Note also that you are doing a considerable amount of walking and some backtracking. Don't be dismayed; the extra walking will literally save you as much as two hours of standing in line. But remember, during the morning do not dally between rides.

DIRECTION	EXPLANATION
12. After seeing the *Country Bear Jamboree*, go to the Frontierland Railroad Station and catch the train for a ride around the perimeter of the park. If the Magic Kingdom is open past 6 P.M., disembark at the Main Street Station, exit the park (having your hand stamped for return entry if necessary) and board the monorail to the Contemporary Resort Hotel for a relaxing lunch. If the park closes early or if you don't feel like eating continue on the train to the Main Street Station and proceed to the next step.	The Walt Disney World Railroad is a fast-loading, high-capacity transportation ride. If the park is open late, or if you are making fairly good progress, get out of the crowd and go to the Contemporary Resort Hotel for lunch. Since the Magic Kingdom (and its restaurants) is busiest between 11:30 A.M. and 2:30 P.M., these times are often slack at the Resort Hotels. In timed experiments, our researchers have exited the park for lunch at the Contemporary Resort Hotel and returned in less time than it took (due to long waiting lines) to obtain and eat a fast-food lunch inside the

DIRECTION	EXPLANATION
	park. An extra bonus at the Resort Hotels is the availability of wine, beer, and mixed drinks.
13. Having arrived back at Main Street Station following lunch at the Contemporary Resort Hotel (or, having arrived from Frontierland if you elected not to eat), see the *Walt Disney Story* on Main Street.	Main Street will not be crowded at this time.
14. Visit the Swiss Family Island Treehouse in Adventureland if the lines are not beyond the entrance turnstile. Otherwise go on to Step 15.	Lines vary throughout the middle of the day at this attraction. See it if lines are tolerable, otherwise bypass it until later.
15. While in Adventureland, check to see when the next performance of the *Tropical Serenade* is scheduled. If you will have to wait more than fifteen minutes, go on to Step 16 and then come back. If the estimated wait is fifteen minutes or less, stay and see the show.	The *Tropical Serenade (Enchanted Tiki Birds)* usually accommodates all, or at least the majority, of those waiting in line at the next performance.
16. While in Adventureland, see Pirates of the Caribbean.	Do not be dismayed if the lines here appear long. Pirates of the Caribbean is one of the fastest-loading rides in the park.
17. There is a shortcut to Frontierland opposite the Swiss Family Island Treehouse. Restrooms and phones are situated along the corridor of this shortcut, so just follow the signs. Emerging in Frontierland next to the Diamond	Go to Liberty Square via the Adventureland-Frontierland connector and see the Hall of Presidents if you missed it earlier.

DIRECTION	EXPLANATION
Horseshoe Saloon, proceed to Liberty Square and see the Hall of Presidents if you missed it earlier.	
18. If the park is open later than 7 P.M., ride the Liberty Square Riverboat. If the park closes at 7 P.M. or earlier, skip the boat ride for the time being.	The riverboat accommodates a large number of people but takes a long time to load and unload. If the park closes early, bypass the boat for now and come back later if you have time.
19. Return to Fantasyland and ride It's a Small World.	Don't worry if the line looks long; the ride loads quickly and your wait will be tolerable.
20. Try to catch a performance of the *Fantasy Follies* at the Fantasyland Theater opposite Cinderella's Golden Carousel.	Schedule of performances is posted outside the theater.
21. Option: If the line is not too long (beyond the entrance gate), take the Skyway to Tomorrowland. If the line is long, exit Fantasyland through Cinderella Castle and proceed to Tomorrowland.	Proceed to Tomorrowland via the Skyway or on foot.
22. In Tomorrowland see *American Journeys.*	This is a large-capacity show for which your wait should be short.
23. After *American Journeys* take in the Mission to Mars.	This is an average-capacity theater attraction which should not be particularly crowded in mid-to-late afternoon when you arrive.
24. Ride If You Had Wings.	A continuous-loading ride with high carrying capacity.

DIRECTION	EXPLANATION
25. Next ride the WEDway PeopleMover, also in Tomorrowland. This ride, among other things, will take you into the interior of Space Mountain where you can observe the crowd situation.	A high-carrying-capacity, well-engineered ride. Check out the line in Space Mountain as you ride through.
26. Try the Carousel of Progress, once again in Tomorrowland.	A high-capacity theater.
27. Then, ride Space Mountain. If you have a lot of time remaining before the closing time and Space Mountain (from your WEDway PeopleMover observation) is crowded, go back and see some of the attractions you missed earlier, returning to ride Space Mountain during the forty minutes before Tomorrowland closes.	Space Mountain stays busy most of the day. The best times to ride are first thing in the morning and during the hour before closing. If Space Mountain is one of your top Magic Kingdom priorities, ride it first and then proceed with the rest of the Touring Plan as outlined.
	During the hour before the park closes, Space Mountain visitors are held in line outside the entrance until all those previously in line have ridden, thus emptying the attraction inside. The appearance from the outside is that the waiting line is enormous, when in reality, the only persons waiting are those visible in front of the entrance. This crowd-control technique, known as "stacking," has the effect of dissuading visitors from riding because they perceive the line to be too long (when in fact the whole line consists only of those standing outside the entrance). Stacking is used in several Walt Disney World rides and attractions during the hour

DIRECTION	EXPLANATION
	before closing as a mechanism for insuring that the attraction will be able to close on schedule. For those who are not scared away by the apparently long lines, the waiting period is usually short.
28. If you have some time left before closing, backtrack to pick up attractions you may have missed, or have bypassed because the lines were too long. Save Main Street until last since it stays open an hour after the rest of the park closes.	
29. Continue to tour until everything closes except Main Street. Finish your day browsing Main Street until you are ready to leave the park.	Main Street is beautiful in the evening with the lights on—it is also very crowded. The shops will be packed, but it is better to shop at the end of the day than to waste valuable time before you have completed your touring.
30. Assuming that you drove to Walt Disney World or have to catch a shuttle back to your hotel, you will take the monorail back to the Transportation and Ticket Center.	Not unexpectedly, the monorail back to the Transportation and Ticket Center is packed. Beat the crowds by taking a monorail to the Contemporary Resort Hotel and reboarding there (transferring if needed) for the Transportation and Ticket Center.

— Outline of Magic Kingdom One-Day Touring Plan for Adults —

1. Arrive at the parking area one hour and fifteen minutes before the stated opening time of the park.
2. Take the monorail from the Transportation and Ticket Center to the Magic Kingdom.
3. Stop at City Hall on Main Street for a schedule of the day's live entertainment and special events. These live performances, with the exception of the *Fantasy Follies*, will not be included in Magic Kingdom One-Day Touring Plan. You may, however, wish to substitute a particular performance or event for one of the attractions specified in the Touring Plan. At fifteen minutes before the park's stated opening time, proceed to the central hub and wait to be admitted to the rest of the park.
4. Go to Adventureland—ride the Jungle Cruise.
5. Go to Frontierland—ride Big Thunder Mountain Railroad.
6. Go to Fantasyland—ride 20,000 Leagues Under the Sea.
7. While in Fantasyland—ride Snow White's Scary Adventures.
8. While in Fantasyland—ride Peter Pan's Flight.
9. Go to Liberty Square—see the Haunted Mansion.
10. While in Liberty Square—see the Hall of Presidents if the wait for the next show does not exceed fifteen minutes; otherwise proceed to Step 11.
11. Go to Frontierland—see the *Country Bear Jamboree*.
12. Go to Frontierland Train Station—ride the railroad around the park perimeter, disembarking at Main Street. Exit the park and take the monorail to the Contemporary Resort Hotel for lunch. Return via monorail to the Magic Kingdom and proceed to Step 13. If you elected not to leave the park for lunch proceed directly to Step 13.
13. While on Main Street—see the *Walt Disney Story*.
14. Go to Adventureland—tour the Swiss Family Island Treehouse if the lines do not extend beyond the entrance turnstile; otherwise go to Step 15.
15. While in Adventureland—see the *Tropical Serenade (Enchanted*

Tiki Birds) if the wait does not exceed fifteen minutes; otherwise go to Step 16 and then return to the *Tropical Serenade*.

16. While in Adventureland—tour Pirates of the Caribbean.

17. Return to Liberty Square—see the Hall of Presidents if you missed it earlier; otherwise go to Step 18.

18. While in Liberty Square—if the park is open past 7 P.M. ride the Liberty Square Riverboat; if the park closes at 7 P.M. or earlier, skip the Riverboat for the time being.

19. Return to Fantasyland—ride It's a Small World.

20. While in Fantasyland—try to catch a performance of the *Fantasy Follies* in the Fantasyland Theater; bypass if the wait exceeds thirty minutes.

21. Go to Tomorrowland—take the Skyway from Fantasyland if the line does not extend past the Skyway entrance gate. If the line is long, exit Fantasyland through Cinderella Castle and proceed to Tomorrowland on foot.

22. In Tomorrowland—see *American Journeys*.

23. In Tomorrowland—experience the Mission to Mars.

24. In Tomorrowland—ride If You Had Wings.

25. In Tomorrowland—ride the WEDway PeopleMover; note how busy Space Mountain is as the PeopleMover passes through.

26. In Tomorrowland—see the Carousel of Progress.

27. In Tomorrowland—ride Space Mountain. If Space Mountain is crowded and you have more than an hour before the park closes, visit any attractions you missed during the course of the day. Return to Space Mountain about forty minutes before Tomorrowland is scheduled to close.

28. If you have any time left before the park closes, visit attractions you missed earlier in the day. Do not waste time on Main Street since it stays open an hour later than the rest of the Magic Kingdom.

29. Continue to tour until everything closes except Main Street. Browse Main Street until you are ready to depart the Magic Kingdom.

30. Avoid lines at the monorail station by taking the less crowded monorail to the Contemporary Resort Hotel and transferring (if needed) to a monorail which stops at the Transportation and Ticket Center.

What You Missed

In one day, particularly if the park closes early, it is almost impossible to see and do everything. In the Magic Kingdom One-Day

Touring Plan, we have bypassed certain rides and other features that, in our opinion, are expendable if you are on a tight (one-day) schedule. If, however, you are curious about what you would be missing, here's the list:

Main Street:	Main Street Cinema
	Main Street Vehicles
Adventureland:	Nothing missed
Frontierland:	*Diamond Horseshoe Revue*
	Davy Crockett's Explorer Canoes
	Tom Sawyer Island
	Ft. Sam Clemens
	Frontierland Shootin' Gallery
Liberty Square:	Mike Fink Keelboats
Fantasyland:	Mr. Toad's Wild Ride
	Cinderella's Golden Carousel
	Mad Tea Party
	Dumbo, the Flying Elephant
Tomorrowland:	Grand Prix Raceway
	StarJets
Other:	Live shows and parades, etc., for which no reservations are required. These are all worthwhile. Pick up a schedule of shows and activities at City Hall when you enter the park; you may choose to substitute a parade or show for a feature listed on the Touring Plan.

For additional information about rides, shows, and features both included and excluded from this Touring Plan, see "Part Three, The Magic Kingdom."

FOR: **Parents with children between 4 and 8 years of age**.

ASSUMES: Periodic stops for rest, restrooms, and refreshment.

This Touring Plan represents a compromise between the observed tastes of adults and the observed tastes of younger children. Included in this Touring Plan are many amusement park rides which children may have the opportunity to experience (although in less exotic surroundings) at local fairs and amusement parks. Though these rides are included in the Touring Plan, we suggest, nevertheless, that they be omitted if possible. Often requiring long waits in line, these so-called cycle-loading rides consume valuable touring time. Specifically we refer to:

Mad Tea Party   Dumbo, the Flying Elephant
Cinderella's Golden Carousel   StarJets

This time could be better spent experiencing the many attractions which best demonstrate the Disney creative genius and are only found in the Magic Kingdom.

This Touring Plan is presented in outline form only. For elaboration of the rationale of the different steps see the EXPLANATION column of the Magic Kingdom One-Day Touring Plan, pages 91–97. For critical evaluation of the individual attractions, see "Part Three, The Magic Kingdom," pages 47–65.

Be forewarned that this plan requires a lot of walking and some backtracking; this is necessary to avoid long waits in line. A little extra walking will save you from two to three hours of standing in line. Note also that you may not complete the tour. How far you get will depend on how quickly you move from ride to ride, how many times you pause for rest or food, how quickly and how full the park fills, and what time the park closes. With a little hustle and some luck, it is possible to complete the Touring Plan even on a busy day when the park closes early.

1. Arrive at the main parking lot at least one hour and fifteen minutes before the stated opening time.

2. Take the monorail from the Transportation and Ticket Center to the Magic Kingdom.

3. Stop at City Hall on Main Street (to your immediate left as you pass under the Main Street Station) and obtain a schedule of live entertainment and special events for the day. These will not be included in the Touring Plan, but you may wish to substitute some special performance for a particular step in the Touring Plan. Proceed to the end of Main Street fifteen minutes before the remainder of the park opens and wait to be admitted.

4. Go to Adventureland—ride the Jungle Cruise.

5. Go to Frontierland—ride the Big Thunder Mountain Railroad (this ride is of the roller coaster genre but is more scenic and fun than wild and intimidating; in other words, a fun experience but a "cream puff" roller coaster).

6. Go to Fantasyland—ride 20,000 Leagues Under the Sea.

7. While in Fantasyland—ride Snow White's Scary Adventures.

8. While in Fantasyland—ride Peter Pan's Flight.

9. While in Fantasyland—ride Cinderella's Golden Carousel.

10. While in Fantasyland—ride Dumbo, the Flying Elephant.

11. While in Fantasyland—ride Mr. Toad's Wild Ride.

12. Go to Tomorrowland—ride the Grand Prix Raceway.

13. Try the Tomorrowland Terrace for lunch; the food is more reasonable than in most of the Magic Kingdom eateries. In addition, the service is more efficient and the seating more plentiful.

14. While in Tomorrowland—ride the WEDway PeopleMover.

15. While in Tomorrowland—see the Carousel of Progress.

16. While in Tomorrowland—ride If You Had Wings.

17. While in Tomorrowland—ride the Mission to Mars.

18. Ride the Skyway to Fantasyland if the lines are not long; otherwise, proceed to Fantasyland via the central hub and Cinderella Castle.

19. While in Fantasyland—ride It's a Small World.

20. While in Fantasyland—see the *Fantasy Follies* if a performance is soon scheduled to begin, otherwise, bypass for the time being.

21. Go to Liberty Square—tour the Haunted Mansion.

22. Go to Frontierland—see *Country Bear Jamboree.*

23. Take the connector from Frontierland to Adventureland (follow the signs in Frontierland to the restrooms).

24. In Adventureland—tour Pirates of the Caribbean.

25. Go back to Frontierland—take the raft to Tom Sawyer Island.

26. Depending on your pace, the park attendance, your children's stamina, and whether the park closes early, you may be running out of time. If so, choose one of the following options:
    a. Cross by raft back to Frontierland, go to the Frontierland Railroad Station and take the Walt Disney World Railroad back to Main Street, or
    b. Walk back to Main Street via Adventureland and tour the Swiss Family Island Treehouse en route.
27. If you were able to move swiftly and have some time left, you might:
    a. Cross by raft back to Frontierland from Tom Sawyer Island and ride the Liberty Square Riverboat.
    b. Go back to Frontierland—go to the Frontierland Railroad Station and ride the Walt Disney World Railroad a full circuit around the park, disembarking at Frontierland where you boarded.
    c. Go to Adventureland—tour the Swiss Family Island Treehouse.
28. Go to Main Street—tour and browse until the park closes or until you are ready to exit the park.
29. Return to the Transportation and Ticket Center via the monorail. To avoid the crowds, take the monorail to the Contemporary Resort Hotel, and then, if necessary, transfer to a monorail going to the Transportation and Ticket Center.

What You Missed

Listed below is a summary of the rides, shows, and attractions you will not see on this Magic Kingdom One-Day Touring Plan:

Main Street:	*Walt Disney Story*
	Main Street Cinema
	Main Street Vehicles
Adventureland:	*Tropical Serenade*
Frontierland:	*Diamond Horseshoe Revue*
	Davy Crockett's Explorer Canoes
	Frontierland Shootin' Gallery
	Ft. Sam Clemens
	Hall of Presidents
Liberty Square:	Mike Fink Keelboats

Fantasyland:	Mad Tea Party
Tomorrowland:	Space Mountain
	StarJets
	American Journeys
Other:	Live shows and parades, etc., for which no reservations are required. These are all worthwhile. Pick up a schedule of shows and activities at City Hall when you enter the park; you may choose to substitute a parade or show for a feature listed on the Touring Plan.

── Outline of Magic Kingdom One-Day Touring Plan, for Mature Adults ──

FOR: **Mature visitors who wish to see as much as possible in one day while minimizing standing in line and walking.**

ASSUMES: Stops for rest, food, and refreshment and a willingness to experience new things.

Minimizing walking and seeing most of the Magic Kingdom in one day is a contradiction in terms on a busy day. For this reason, this Touring Plan for mature visitors is more selective in attractions visited. Thus, by following this Touring Plan, you will see those features which are preeminent in the Magic Kingdom plus those less famous features which are especially appreciated by the more mature audience. Further elaboration of the rationale for this Touring Plan can be obtained by referring to the EXPLANATION column in the elaborated version of Magic Kingdom One-Day Touring Plan. Further detail on individual rides, shows, and features can be found in "Part Three, The Magic Kingdom."

1. Arrive at the main parking lot at least one hour and fifteen minutes before the stated opening time.
2. Take the monorail from the Transportation and Ticket Center to the Magic Kingdom.
3. Stop at City Hall on Main Street (to your immediate left as you pass under the Main Street Station) and obtain a schedule of live entertainment and special events for the day. These will not be included in the Touring Plan, but you may wish to substitute some special performance for a particular step in the Touring Plan.
4. Proceed quickly to end of Main Street and wait to be admitted to the rest of the park.
5. When the rest of the park opens walk posthaste to Adventureland and ride the Jungle Cruise.
6. As quickly as possible, leave Adventureland the same way you came in, and proceed through Cinderella Castle to Fantasyland. This will be the one, great, forced march of the day, and though not convenient, will save you as many as two hours of standing in line.

7. In Fantasyland—ride 20,000 Leagues Under the Sea.

8. In Fantasyland—ride Snow White's Scary Adventures.

9. In Fantasyland—ride Peter Pan's Flight (this is one of the attractions most enjoyed by mature audiences).

10. In Fantasyland—ride It's a Small World.

11. Return to Liberty Square—tour the Haunted Mansion.

12. In Liberty Square—see the Hall of Presidents.

13. Proceed to Frontierland—see *Country Bear Jamboree*.

14. Go to Frontierland Railroad Station—ride the railroad around the park perimeter, disembarking at Main Street. Exit the park and take the monorail to the Contemporary Resort Hotel for lunch. Return via monorail after lunch to the Magic Kingdom and proceed to Step 15. If you elected not to leave the park for lunch proceed directly to Step 15.

15. While on Main Street—see the *Walt Disney Story*.

16. Go to Adventureland—tour the Swiss Family Island Treehouse if the lines do not extend beyond the entrance turnstile, and if you think you can handle a little climbing up and down stairs; otherwise, go to Step 17.

17. While in Adventureland—see the *Tropical Serenade (Enchanted Tiki Birds)* if the wait does not exceed fifteen minutes. Otherwise go to Step 18 and then return to the *Tropical Serenade*.

18. While in Adventureland—tour Pirates of the Caribbean.

19. Return to Frontierland (there is a shortcut opposite the Swiss Family Island Treehouse—follow signs to the restrooms), and from there walk to Liberty Square.

20. In Liberty Square—ride the Liberty Square Riverboat.

21. Return to Fantasyland—try to catch a performance of the *Fantasy Follies* in the Fantasyland Theater.

22. Go to Tomorrowland—take the Skyway from Fantasyland if the line does not extend past the Skyway entrance gate. If the line is long, exit Fantasyland via the entrance of Cinderella Castle and proceed to Tomorrowland on foot.

23. In Tomorrowland—see *American Journeys*.

24. In Tomorrowland—experience the Mission to Mars.

25. In Tomorrowland—ride If You Had Wings.

26. In Tomorrowland—ride the WEDway PeopleMover.

27. In Tomorrowland—see the Carousel of Progress.

28. Continue to tour until everything closes except Main Street. Then

browse Main Street until you are ready to depart the Magic Kingdom.

29. Avoid lines at the monorail station by taking the less crowded monorail to the Contemporary Resort Hotel and transferring (if necessary) to a monorail which stops at the Transportation and Ticket Center.

What You Missed

In one day, particularly if the park closes early, it is almost impossible to see and do everything. In this Magic Kingdom One-Day Touring Plan, we have bypassed certain rides and other features which, in our opinion, are expendable if you are on a tight (one-day) schedule. If, however, you are curious about what you would be missing, here's the list:

Main Street:	Main Street Vehicles
	Main Street Cinema
Adventureland:	Nothing missed
Frontierland:	Big Thunder Mountain Railroad
	Tom Sawyer Island
	Diamond Horseshoe Revue
	Davy Crockett's Explorer Canoes
	Ft. Sam Clemens
	Frontierland Shootin' Gallery
Liberty Square:	Mike Fink Keelboats
Fantasyland:	Mad Tea Party
	Mr. Toad's Wild Ride
	Dumbo, the Flying Elephant
	Cinderella's Golden Carousel
Tomorrowland:	StarJets
	Space Mountain
	Grand Prix Raceway
Other:	Live shows and parades, etc., for which no reservations are required. These are all worthwhile. Pick up a schedule of shows and activities at City Hall when you enter the park; you may choose to substitute a parade or show for a feature listed on the Touring Plan.

— *Not to be Missed at the Magic Kingdom* —

Adventureland	Jungle Cruise
	Pirates of the Caribbean
Frontierland	Big Thunder Mountain Railroad
	Country Bear Jamboree
Liberty Square	The Hall of Presidents
	The Haunted Mansion
Fantasyland	It's a Small World
	Peter Pan's Flight
	20,000 Leagues Under the Sea
Tomorrowland	Space Mountain
Special events	Great Main Street Electrical Parade

Magic Kingdom Summary

P.O. Box 40, Lake Buena Vista, FL 32380   Phone: (305) 824-4321
Call ahead for opening/closing times
Type: Fantasy/Adventure Theme Park

Admission Costs

Ticket options	Adults	Children	Discounts	
One-Day Ticket	$18	$15	Children (3–17)	yes
3-Day World Passport	$45	$37	Children under 3	free
4-Day World Passport	$55	$45	Student	no
5-Day World Passport	$65	$53	Military	no
1-Year World Passport	$135	$110	Senior citizens	no
			Group rates	yes

Credit cards accepted for admission: **MasterCard and American Express**
Features included: **All except Frontierland Shootin' Gallery**

*Overall Appeal**

By age groups	Preschool	Grade School	Teens	Young Adults	Over 30	Senior Citizens
	*****	*****	*****	*****	*****	*****

Touring Tips

Touring time	Periods of lightest attendance
Average: **Full day**	Time of day: **Early morning**
Minimum: Full day	Days: **Friday, Sunday**
Touring strategy: **See narrative**	Times of year: **After Thanksgiving**
Rainy day touring: **recommended**	**until 18th of December**

What the Critics Say

Rating of major features:
See pages 45–87

Rating of functional and operational areas

Parking	*****
Restrooms	*****
Resting places	*****
Crowd management	*****
Aesthetic appeal of grounds	*****
Cleanliness/maintenance	*****

Services and Facilities

Restaurant/snack bar **Yes**	Lockers **Yes**
Vending machines (food/pop) **No**	Pet kennels **Yes**
Alcoholic beverages **No**	Gift shops **Yes**
Handicapped access **Yes**	Film sales **Yes**
Wheelchairs **Rental**	Rain check **No**
Baby strollers **Rental**	Private guided group tours **Yes**

* Critical ratings are based on a scale of zero to five stars with five stars being the best possible rating.

PART FOUR—EPCOT Center

— Contrasting EPCOT Center
and the Magic Kingdom —

EPCOT Center is more than twice the physical size of the Magic Kingdom, and it has lines every bit as long as those waiting for the Jungle Cruise or Space Mountain. Obviously, visitors must come prepared to do a considerable amount of walking from attraction to attraction within EPCOT Center and a comparable amount of standing in line.

The size and scope of EPCOT Center also means that one can't really see the whole place in one day without skipping an attraction or two and giving other areas a cursory glance. A major difference between the Magic Kingdom and EPCOT Center, however, is that some of the EPCOT attractions can be either lingered over or skimmed, depending on one's personal interest. A good example is the General Motors' World of Motion pavilion consisting of two sections. The first section is a fifteen-minute ride while the second section is a collection of educational walk-through exhibits and mini-theaters. Nearly all visitors opt to take the ride, but many people, due to time constraints or lack of interest, bypass the exhibits.

Generally speaking, the rides at the Magic Kingdom tend to be designed to create an experience of adventure or fantasy. The experiences created in the EPCOT Center attractions tend to be oriented towards education or inspiration.

Some people will find that the attempts at education are superficial; others will want more entertainment and less education. Most visitors are somewhere in between, finding plenty of entertainment **and** education.

In any event, EPCOT Center is more of an adult place than the Magic Kingdom. What it gains in taking a futuristic, visionary, and technological look at the world, it loses, just a bit, in warmth, happiness, and charm.

As in the Magic Kingdom, we have identified several attractions in EPCOT Center as "not to be missed." But part of the enjoyment of a place like EPCOT Center is that there is something for everyone. If you go in a group, no doubt there will be quite a variety of opinions as to which attraction is "best."

—— *Arriving and Getting Oriented* ——

Arriving at EPCOT Center by private automobile is easy and direct. The park has its own parking lot, and unlike the Magic Kingdom, there is no need to take a monorail or ferryboat to reach the entrance. Trams serve the entire EPCOT Center lot, or if you wish you can walk to the front gate. Monorail service does connect EPCOT Center with the Magic Kingdom parking lot, the Magic Kingdom (transfer required), and with the Polynesian Village and Contemporary Resort Hotels (transfer also required).

Like the Magic Kingdom, EPCOT Center has theme sections, but only two: Future World and World Showcase. The technological talent of major corporations and the creative talent of Disney Enterprises went into Future World, which represents a look at where man has come from and where he is going. World Showcase, featuring the distinctive landmarks, cuisine, and culture of a number of nations, is meant to be a sort of permanent world's fair.

From the standpoint of finding your way around, however, EPCOT Center is not at all like the Magic Kingdom. The Magic Kingdom is designed so that at nearly any location in the park you feel a part of a very specific environment—Liberty Square, let's say, or Main Street, U.S.A. Each of these environments is visually closed off from other parts of the park to preserve the desired atmosphere. It wouldn't do for the Jungle Cruise to pass the roaring blacktop of the Grand Prix Raceway, for example.

EPCOT Center, by contrast, is visually open. And while it seems strange to see Liberty Hall on the same horizon with the Eiffel Tower, in-park navigation is normally simplified. A possible exception is in Future World where the enormous east and west CommuniCore buildings effectively hide everything on their opposite sides.

While Cinderella Castle is the focal landmark of the Magic Kingdom, Spaceship Earth is the architectural symbol of EPCOT Center. This shiny, 180-foot "geosphere" is visible from almost every point. Like Cinderella Castle, it can help you keep track of where you are in the park. But because it's in a high-traffic location, and because it's not centrally located, it does not make a very good meeting place.

Any of the distinctively designed national pavilions make good meeting places, but be more specific than, "Hey, let's meet in Japan!" That may sound fun and catchy but remember that the national pavilions are mini-towns, with buildings, monuments, gardens, and plazas. You could wander around quite awhile "in Japan" without making connections with your group. Pick out a specific place in Japan, the sidewalk side of the pagoda, for example.

More Information and Help Galore— WorldKey Information Service

Whether you need more information or assistance or not, you should know about the innovative WorldKey Information Service. It not only may be useful as you visit EPCOT Center, it will also give you some experience dealing with what may be one of the common video systems of the future.

WorldKey is a network of interactive video display terminals—televisions that react when you touch certain parts of the screen.

The WorldKey system, developed by the Bell System and Walt Disney Productions, will provide you with up to forty minutes of information about EPCOT Center, showing maps and pictures, and describing attractions, restaurants, entertainment, guest services, and shops.

Be patient with the WorldKey and it will guide you, step by step, through an explanation of how to use the system—in English or in Spanish (French and German are to be added later). Stick with the program through at least a few steps and you can use the WorldKey to contact an attendant. Via two-way television and hands-free two-way speakers, the WorldKey attendant can answer your questions, make hotel or restaurant reservations, and help find lost children, among other things.

Because the WorldKey system is so novel, a lot of visitors "play" with it as though it were just another video game. For most people this play is actually an educational experience. They are using what could become one of the data retrieval systems of tomorrow. They are learning about touch-sensitive screens. (You don't need to press, by the way; sometimes the system reacts even before your finger touches the screen.)

But whether people play with the WorldKey or put it to work, they usually end up walking away from the screen without completing the WorldKey program and setting it up for the next user. If people get frustrated with the WorldKey it's usually because they walked up to it while it was in the middle of showing the last user what he asked to see. Touch the yellow square and you'll get back to the beginning of the program.

If, as opposed to finding a program in progress left from a previous user, you initiate the program, the WorldKey will quickly show you, step by step, how to use the system.

If you wish to speak to an attendant, work through the program until a small picture of an attendant is displayed on the screen. Touch the attendant's picture and soon one of the WorldKey attendants will come "live" onto the screen, ready to communicate with you. You can make restaurant reservations at this time and avoid standing in line for reservations at the places themselves.

Future World

Gleaming, futuristic structures of immense proportions leave little in doubt concerning the orientation of this, the first encountered theme area of EPCOT Center. The thoroughfares are broad and punctuated with billowing fountains, reflected in the shining facades of space-age architecture. Everything, including the bountiful landscaping, is clean and sparkling to the point of asepsis and seemingly bigger than life. Pavilions dedicated to man's past, present, and future technological accomplishments form the perimeter of the Future World area with the Spaceship Earth and its flanking CommuniCores East and West standing preeminent front and center.

Spaceship Earth

DESCRIPTION AND COMMENTS   This Bell System ride spirals through the seventeen-story interior of EPCOT Center's premier landmark, taking visitors past Audio-Animatronics scenes depicting man's developments in communications, from cave painting to printing to television to space communications and computer networks. The ride is compelling and well done as you ascend the geosphere but, to us, a little disappointing on the way back down. Even so, it's a masterpiece and is thus accorded a "not to be missed" rating.

TOURING TIPS   This is probably the toughest attraction in EPCOT Center to see without literally investing hours of your time standing in line. The only way we know to beat the crowd at Spaceship Earth is to be one of the first visitors in the park when it opens. If lines are long when you arrive, try again between 5:30 P.M. and 6:30 P.M. Do not miss it, however, even if you have to stand awhile in line; it's one of Disney's prize achievements.

Earth Station

DESCRIPTION AND COMMENTS   Not an attraction as such. Earth Station is situated at the base of the geosphere and serves as the exit of Spaceship Earth. It also serves as EPCOT Center's primary guest relations and information center. Attendants staff information booths and a number of WorldKey terminals are available. If you have spent any time in the Magic Kingdom, Earth Station is EPCOT Center's version of City Hall.

TOURING TIPS If you wish to eat in one of the EPCOT Center sit-down restaurants, you can make your reservations from Earth Station through a WorldKey Information Service attendant (instead of running to the restaurant itself and standing in line for reservations, which is another alternative). See the description of the WorldKey system, page 115, and the section dealing with eating in EPCOT Center, page 142.

CommuniCore

DESCRIPTION AND COMMENTS The name stands for "Community Core," and it consists of two huge, crescent-shaped, glass-walled structures housing industry-sponsored walk-through and "hands-on" exhibits, restaurants, and a gift shop. The Disney people like to describe it as a "twenty-first century village square where the town crier is an array of computer-fed, interactive, video screens and high technology electronics libraries."

TOURING TIPS CommuniCore (two buildings: east and west) provides visitors an opportunity to sample a variety of technology in a fun, "hands-on" manner through the use of various interactive communication devices. Some of the exhibits are quite intriguing while others are a little dry. We observed a wide range of reactions by visitors to the many CommuniCore exhibits and can only suggest that you form your own opinion. In terms of touring strategy, we suggest you spend time in CommuniCore on your second day at EPCOT Center. If you only have one day, visit sometime during the evening if you have time. Be warned, however, that CommuniCore exhibits are almost all technical and educational in nature and may not be compatible with your mood or level of energy toward the end of a long day of touring. Also be advised that you cannot get much of anything out of a quick walk-through of CommuniCore; you have to play with the equipment to understand what is going on.

Attractions in CommuniCore include:

Travelport

DESCRIPTION AND COMMENTS This American Express exhibit in CommuniCore West has "vacation stations" equipped with touch-sensitive video terminals similar to those in the WorldKey system. If you work with a terminal you can see different types of vacations in different geographical areas.

TOURING TIPS   See comments in CommuniCore Touring Tips.

Energy Exchange

DESCRIPTION AND COMMENTS   There are also touch-sensitive video terminals in this Exxon exhibit, permitting users to tap into information about a variety of energy topics. Stationary displays are devoted to specific energy sources—solar, coal, nuclear, oil, and others. Visitors can use some of the devices to demonstrate the generation and expenditure of energy.

TOURING TIPS   See comments in CommuniCore Touring Tips.

EPCOT Computer Central

DESCRIPTION AND COMMENTS   Touch-sensitive video terminals show users through simple and entertaining games how computers are used in design and control. A robot called SMRT-1 plays guessing games with guests by decoding yes and no answers through a voice recognition box.

TOURING TIPS   See comments in CommuniCore Touring Tips.

Backstage Magic

DESCRIPTION AND COMMENTS   This Sperry exhibit gives visitors a look through the windows of the EPCOT Center Computer Control Room.

TOURING TIPS   This exhibit is produced in a small theater, so there is almost always a minimum wait in line of twenty minutes. The show is not particularly compelling or informative; one of EPCOT Center's less appealing offerings in our opinion.

FutureCom

DESCRIPTION AND COMMENTS   A Bell System exhibit with a variety of electronic games demonstrating facets of telecommunications. Another part of the exhibit demonstrates video teleconferencing, putting visitors face-to-face via two-way television with an attendant. Still another section has touch-sensitive video terminals that enable guests to "call up" information on any U.S. state and its current events.

TOURING TIPS   See comments in CommuniCore Touring Tips.

Electronic Forum

DESCRIPTION AND COMMENTS   This section of CommuniCore consists of World News Center, which has TV monitors carrying live news broadcasts from around the world. At Future Choice Theater visitors can participate in an on-going opinion poll by pushing buttons built into the armrests of their seats. Responses appear on the theater screen so guests can see how their opinions stack up against those of other visitors.

TOURING TIPS   See comments in CommuniCore Touring Tips.

The Living Seas

DESCRIPTION AND COMMENTS   The Living Seas is the newest and one of the most ambitious Future World offerings. The focus is a huge, 200-foot diameter, 27-foot deep main tank containing approximately 2,000 fish, mammals, and crustaceans in a simulation of a real ocean ecosystem. Scientists and divers conduct actual marine experiments underwater in view of EPCOT Center guests. Visitors can view the undersea activity from an observation bubble atop the tank, through 8-inch-thick viewing windows below the surface (including viewing windows in the Coral Reef Restaurant), and via a three-part adventure/ride which is the featured attraction of The Living Seas. This last consists of a movie dramatizing the link between the ocean and man's survival followed by an elevator descent to the bottom of the tank. Here guests board gondolas for a three-minute voyage through an underwater viewing tunnel.

TOURING TIPS   Anything new at EPCOT Center draws crowds which are larger than normal.* Either go before 10:30 A.M. or after 5 P.M.

The Land

DESCRIPTION AND COMMENTS   The Land is in fact a huge pavilion sponsored by Kraft which contains three attractions (discussed next) and a number of restaurants.

* Open as of January 15, 1986.

TOURING TIPS   The Land is a good place for a fast-food lunch; if you are there to see the attraction, however, don't go during meal times.

Attractions in The Land include:

Listen to the Land

DESCRIPTION AND COMMENTS   A boat ride which takes visitors through a simulated giant seed germination, past various inhospitable environments man has faced as a farmer, and through a futuristic, innovative greenhouse where real crops are being grown using the latest agricultural technologies. Inspiring and educational with excellent effects and a good narrative, this attraction should "not be missed."

TOURING TIPS   This "not to be missed" attraction should be seen before the lunch crowd hits The Land restaurants, i.e., before 11:30 A.M., or alternatively in the evening after 6:30 P.M.

Kitchen Kabaret

DESCRIPTION AND COMMENTS   Disney Audio-Animatronics (robotic) characters in the forms of various foods and kitchen appliances take the stage in an educational musical revue which tells the story of the basic food groups (protein, carbohydrates, etc.). It's a cute show with entertainment provided by such characters as Bonnie Appetit, the Cereal Sisters, and the comedy team of Mr. Hamm and Mr. Eggz.

TOURING TIPS   One of the few light entertainment offerings at EPCOT Center. Slightly reminiscent of the *Country Bear Jamboree* in the Magic Kingdom (but not quite as humorous or endearing in our opinion). Though the theater is not large, we have never encountered any long waits at the *Kitchen Kabaret* (even during meal times). Nevertheless, we recommend you go before 11:30 A.M. or after 5 P.M.

Harvest Theater

DESCRIPTION AND COMMENTS   This attraction features a 70mm Panavision film, *Symbiosis*. The subject is the interrelationship of man and his environment, and demonstrates how easily man can upset the ecological balance. The film is superb in its production and not too heavy-handed in its sobering message. The cinematic technique is "state of the art."

TOURING TIPS   This extremely worthwhile film should be part of every visitor's touring day. Long waits are usually not a problem at the

Harvest Theater, but as with *Kitchen Kabaret*, we recommend you go before 11:30 A.M. or after 5 P.M.

Journey into Imagination

DESCRIPTION AND COMMENTS   Another multi-attraction pavilion located on the west side of CommuniCore West and down the walk from The Land. Outside is an "upside-down waterfall" and one of our favorite Future World landmarks, the so-called "jumping water," a leap-frogging fountain that seems to hop over the heads of unsuspecting passers-by.

TOURING TIPS   We recommend early morning or late evening touring. See the individual attractions for further specifics.

Attractions in Journey into Imagination include:

Journey into Imagination Ride

DESCRIPTION AND COMMENTS   This ride introduces two new Disney characters—Figment, an impish purple dragon, and Dreamfinder, a red-bearded adventurer who pilots a contraption designed to search out and capture ideas. This ride, with its happy, humorous orientation and superb Audio-Animatronics and special effects, is one of the most fun and delightful attractions in the park. It is "not to be missed."

TOURING TIPS   This "not to be missed" ride is the big draw in this corner of Future World. We recommend seeing it before 10:30 A.M., or alternatively after 7 P.M.

The Image Works

DESCRIPTION AND COMMENTS   This is a playground for the imagination utilizing light, color, sound, and electronic devices which can be manipulated by visitors. There's the Magic Palette, with a video-screen canvas and an electronic paintbrush. Especially fun is the Electronic Philharmonic which enables visitors to conduct the brass, woodwind, percussion, and string sections of an orchestra by movements of the hand. (The secret is raising and lowering your hands over the labeled discs on the console. Don't try pressing the discs as if they were buttons. Pretend you're a conductor—raise a hand away from the disc labeled brass, for example, and you will get louder brass. Lower your hand toward the disc labeled woodwinds and you'll get less volume from the woodwinds section.)

TOURING TIPS   There are quite a number of interesting things to do and play with here; far more than the representative examples we listed. If you have more than one day at EPCOT Center, save the Image Works for the second day. If you are on a one-day schedule, try to work it in during the evening or alternatively in the morning before 11:30 A.M.

The Magic Eye Theater

DESCRIPTION AND COMMENTS   This theater features a 3-D fantasy film, *Magic Journeys*, which may be the favorite attraction of children visiting EPCOT Center; adults also enjoy it immensely. The production is solid, the theme happy and upbeat, and the 3-D effects incredible. All over the theater children (and many adults) reach out involuntarily to grab objects which seem to be floating out from the screen. The story line deals with a group of children on their flights of imagination. If you enjoy this type of entertainment, Marineland, south of St. Augustine on A-1-A, also has an excellent 3-D movie. Our research team was split concerning which of the two 3-D films is better.

TOURING TIPS   This is a "not to be missed" attraction if there are children in your group, and should probably be a "not to be missed" for adults also. Go before 11:30 A.M. or after 5:30 P.M.

The World of Motion

DESCRIPTION AND COMMENTS   Presented by General Motors, this pavilion is to the left of Spaceship Earth when you enter and down toward World Showcase from the Universe of Energy pavilion. The pavilion is home to It's Fun to Be Free, a ride, and to TransCenter, an assembly of stationary exhibits and mini-theater productions on the theme of transportation.

Attractions in The World of Motion include:
It's Fun to Be Free

DESCRIPTION AND COMMENTS   A "not to be missed" attraction, this ride conducts visitors through a continuum of twenty-four Audio-Animatronics scenes depicting where and how man has traveled, and what the future has in store for travel. The detail-work in individual scenes is amazing and the tongue-in-cheek, humorous tone of the ride makes the history lesson more than tolerable.

TOURING TIPS   This ride has a large carrying capacity and an efficient loading system, keeping lines generally manageable. Many days you can hop on this ride any time you want. Its largest crowds build between noon and 2 P.M. and immediately after an audience has been discharged from Universe of Energy nearby.

TransCenter

DESCRIPTION AND COMMENTS   Most visitors enter TransCenter when they disembark from the ride described above, but there are separate doors on the east side of the pavilion for those who wish to visit the various exhibits without taking the ride. TransCenter is a walk-through attraction of 33,000 square feet, and deals with a wide range of topics relating to transportation. One major display demonstrates the importance of aerodynamics to fuel economy, while others evaluate the prospects of future power systems and explains why the industry is turning to robotic production techniques. Yet another display, Dreamers' Workshop, shows some advanced designs for the possible land, sea, and air conveyances of tomorrow.

TOURING TIPS   There's a lot to see here. How much you take in will be determined by your interest in the subject and the flexibility of your schedule. We like TransCenter on the second day of a two-day visit, or during the mid-afternoon if you enjoy this sort of display more than the offerings of World Showcase. Late evening after you have finished your "must list" is also a good time.

Universe of Energy

DESCRIPTION AND COMMENTS   The Audio-Animatronics dinosaurs and the unique traveling theater make this Exxon pavilion one of the most popular in Future World. Since this is a theater with a ride component, the line does not move at all while the show is in progress. When the theater empties, however, a large chunk of the line will disappear as people are admitted for the next show. At this "not to be missed" attraction, visitors are seated in what appears to be a fairly ordinary theater while they watch an animated film on fossil fuels. Then, the theater seats divide into six, 97-passenger traveling cars which glide among the swamps and reptiles of a prehistoric forest. The special effects include the feel of warm, clammy air from the swamp, the smell of sulphur from an erupting volcano, and the sight of red lava hissing and bubbling towards the passengers. The remainder of the performance utilizes some nifty cinematic techniques to bring you back to the leading edge of energy research and development.

TOURING TIPS   This "not to be missed" attraction draws large crowds beginning early in the morning. Either catch the show before 10:30 A.M. or wait until after 6:30 P.M. Waits for the Universe of Energy are normally within tolerable limits, however, since the Universe of Energy contains two separate theaters which can be operated simultaneously.

Horizons

DESCRIPTION AND COMMENTS   The General Electric pavilion takes a look back at yesterday's visions of the future, including Jules Verne's concept of a moon rocket and a 1930's preview of a neon city. Elsewhere guests visit FuturePort and ride through a family habitat of the next century, with scenes depicting apartment, farm, and underwater and space communities.

TOURING TIPS   The entire Horizons pavilion is devoted to a single, continuously loading ride, which has a large carrying capacity. This "not to be missed" attraction can be enjoyed almost any time of day without long waits in line. An exception occurs immediately following the conclusion of a Universe of Energy performance next door, when up to 580 patrons often troop over and queue up for Horizons en masse. If you chance to encounter this deluge or its aftermath, take a 15-minute break. Chances are when you return to Horizons you will be able to walk right in.

World Showcase

The second theme component of EPCOT Center is World Showcase. Situated around picturesque World Showcase Lagoon, it is an ongoing world's fair, with the cuisine, culture, history, and architecture of almost a dozen countries permanently on display in individual national pavilions. The so-called pavilions, which generally consist of familiar landmarks and typically representative street scenes from the host country, are spaced along a 1.2-mile promenade which circles the impressive forty-acre lagoon. Double-decker omnibuses carry visitors to stops around the promenade, and boats ferry guests across the lagoon (the lines at the bus stops tend to be pushy, however, and it's almost always quicker to walk than to use the buses or the boats). Moving clockwise around the promenade, the nations represented are:

Mexico

DESCRIPTION AND COMMENTS   Two pre-Colombian pyramids dominate the architecture of this exhibit. The first makes up the facade of the pavilion and the second overlooks the restaurant and plaza alongside the boat ride, El Rio del Tiempo, inside the pavilion.

El Rio del Tiempo, The River of Time, is a boat trip which winds among Audio-Animatronics and cinematic scenes depicting the history of Mexico from the ancient cultures of the Maya, Toltec, and Aztec civilizations to modern times. Special effects include fiber-optic projections that provide a spectacular fireworks display near the end of the ride.

TOURING TIPS   A romantic and exciting testimony to the charms of Mexico, this pavilion probably contains more authentic and valuable artifacts and objets d'art than any other national pavilion. Many people zip right past these treasures without even stopping to look. The village scene on the interior of the pavilion is both beautiful and exquisitely detailed. We recommend seeing this pavilion before 11 A.M. and after 7 P.M.

People's Republic of China

DESCRIPTION AND COMMENTS   A half-sized replica of the Temple of Heaven in Beijing (Peking) identifies this pavilion. Gardens and reflecting ponds simulate those found in Suzhou, and an Art Gallery features a "Lotus Blossom" gate and formal saddleridge roof line.

Pass through the Hall of Prayer for Good Harvest to see the Circle-Vision 360 motion picture, *Wonders of China.* Warm and appealing, the film serves as a brilliant introduction to the people and natural beauty of this little known nation. Two restaurants have been added to the China pavilion since its opening, a fast-food eatery and a lovely, reservations-only, full-service establishment.

TOURING TIPS   A truly beautiful pavilion, serene yet exciting. We recommend that you tour before 11:30 A.M. and after 2 P.M.

We recommend the same visitation times for the *Wonders of China*, an excellent film, as for the pavilion in general.

Germany

DESCRIPTION AND COMMENTS   A clocktower adorned with boy and girl figures overlooks the platz, or plaza, which identifies the pavilion of the Federal Republic of Germany. Dominated by a fountain depicting St. George's victory over the dragon, the platz is encircled by buildings reflecting traditional German architecture. A future ride attraction will take visitors through Germany's interconnecting river system of the Rhine, Tauber, Ruhr, and Isar. For the moment, however, the focal attraction is the Biergarten, a full-service (reservations only) restaurant featuring German food and beer. At evening meals only, yodeling, German folk dancing, singing, and oompah band music accompany the fare.

TOURING TIPS   The pavilion is pleasant and festive. Until the river ride is completed Germany is recommended for touring at any time of the day.

Italy

DESCRIPTION AND COMMENTS   The entrance to the Italian pavilion is marked by the 105-foot campanile, or bell tower, said to be a mirror image of the tower that overlooks St. Mark's Square in Venice. To the left of the campanile is a replica of the fourteenth century Doge's Palace, also a Venetian landmark. Other buildings are composites of architecture found throughout Italy. The style is Florentine, for example, for L'Originale Alfredo di Roma Ristorante. Visitors can watch pasta being made in this popular restaurant which specializes in Fettuccine All'Alfredo. The Italian pavilion even has a small Venetian island with gondolas tied to barber-pole-striped moorings at the edge of the World Showcase Lagoon.

TOURING TIPS   The streets and courtyards in the Italian pavilion are among the most realistic in World Showcase—you really feel as if you have been transplanted to Italy. Since there is no attraction (film, ride, etc.) at the Italian pavilion, touring is recommended for all hours.

United States

DESCRIPTION AND COMMENTS   The United States pavilion, generally referred to as *The American Adventure* for the historical production performed there, consists of (typically) a fast-food restaurant and a patriotic, Audio-Animatronics show.

The American Adventure is a composite of everything the Disney people do best. Situated in an almost life-size replica of Philadelphia's Liberty Hall, the production is a stirring, twenty-nine-minute rendition of American history narrated by the Audio-Animatronics figures of Mark Twain (who carries a smoking cigar) and Ben Franklin (who climbs a set of stairs to visit Thomas Jefferson). Behind a stage that's almost half the size of a football field is a 28×155 foot, rear-projection screen (the largest ever used) on which appropriate motion picture images are interwoven with the action occurring on stage. Definitely a "not to be missed" attraction.

TOURING TIPS   Large and patriotic, but not as interesting externally as most of the other pavilions. The Liberty Inn restaurant is one of the few places in the World Showcase to obtain a quick, fast-food meal.

The American Adventure is, in the opinion of our research team, the very best attraction at EPCOT Center. It usually plays to capacity audiences from around noon through 7 P.M., so try to see it early or late. Because of the theater's large capacity, waiting during the busy times of the day would hardly ever approach an hour, and would probably average twenty-five to forty minutes.

Japan

DESCRIPTION AND COMMENTS   The five-story, blue-roofed pagoda, inspired by a shrine built in Nara in the seventh century, sets this pavilion apart from its neighbors. A hill garden rises behind it with arrangements of waterfalls, rocks, flowers, lanterns, paths, and rustic bridges. The building on the right (as one faces the entrance) was inspired by the ceremonial and coronation hall on the Imperial Palace Grounds at Kyoto. It contains restaurants and a large retail store. Passing through the courtyard, one crosses a moat and enters a massive Samurai "castle" that will house Meet the World. This attraction, in which the audience seating area will revolve around the stage, will feature Audio-Animatronics characters in settings that depict Japan's history and spirit.

TOURING TIPS A tasteful and elaborate pavilion which creatively blends simplicity, architectural grandeur, and natural beauty, Japan can be toured at any time of day.

Morocco

DESCRIPTION AND COMMENTS The bustle of the market, narrow, winding streets, lofty minarets, and stuccoed archways recreate the romance and intrigue of Tangiers and Casablanca. Attention to detail makes Morocco one of the most exciting of the World Showcase pavilions. In addition to the bazaar, Morocco also features a museum of Moorish art and the Marrakech Restaurant, which serves some unusual and difficult-to-find North African ethnic specialities.

TOURING TIPS Since there is no ride or theater attraction in Morocco, it can be toured anytime at your convenience.

France

DESCRIPTION AND COMMENTS Naturally there is a replica of the Eiffel Tower (and a big one at that), but the rest of the pavilion is meant to reflect a more general ambience of France in the period 1870 to 1910, a period known as La Belle Epoque (the beautiful time). The sidewalk cafe and the restaurant are both very popular here, but so is the pastry shop. You won't be the first visitor to get the idea of buying a croissant to tide you over until you can obtain a decent meal.

Impressions de France is the name of an eighteen-minute movie which is projected over 200 degrees onto five screens. They let you sit down in France (compared to the standing theaters in China and Canada) to view a well-made film introduction to the people, cities, and natural wonders of France.

TOURING TIPS This pavilion is rich in atmosphere attributable to its detailed street scenes and bygone era flavor.

The streets of the French pavilion are diminutive and become quite congested when visitors line up for the film. Waits in line can be substantial here, so we recommend viewing before noon and after 7 P.M.

United Kingdom

DESCRIPTION AND COMMENTS   A variety of periods and facades, with attempts to create city, town, and rural atmospheres, are compressed into this pavilion, which is mostly shops. The Rose and Crown Pub and Dining Room is the only World Showcase restaurant with dining on the water side of the promenade. A city square, with classic formal facade, copies a look found in London and Edinburgh. One street has a 1500's style thatched-roof cottage, a four-story timber and plaster building, a pre-Georgian plaster building, a formal Palladian exterior of dressed stone, and a city square with Hyde Park bandstand (whew!).

TOURING TIPS   We would have to say that this was our least favorite pavilion—not bad, mind you—we just think it could have been a whole lot better. There are no attractions here to create congestion, so tour at any time you wish. Reservations are not needed to enjoy the Pub section of the Rose and Crown Pub, making it a nice place to stop for a beer long about mid-afternoon.

Canada

DESCRIPTION AND COMMENTS   The cultural, natural, and architectural diversity of the United States' neighbor to the north is reflected in this large and impressive pavilion. Thirty-foot totem poles embellish an Indian village situated beneath the gables of a magnificent château-style hotel. Near the hotel is a rugged stone building said to be modeled after a famous landmark near Niagara Falls, reflective of Canada's British influence. Canada also has a fine film extolling its many national, cultural, and natural virtues. Titled *O Canada!* the film is very enlightening, and demonstrates the immense pride Canadians have in their beautiful country. Visitors leave the theater through Victoria Gardens, inspired by the famed Butchart Gardens of British Columbia.

TOURING TIPS   A large-capacity theater attraction which sees fairly heavy early morning attendance since it is the first pavilion encountered as one travels counter-clockwise around World Showcase Lagoon. We recommend late afternoon or early evening as the best time for viewing the film. Le Cellier, a restaurant serving cafeteria-style on the lower level of the Canadian pavilion, is the only "non-fast-food" restaurant in the World Showcase that does not require reservations.

Still to Come

Planning is under way for Spain, Israel, Venezuela, and equatorial Africa to have pavilions on the World Showcase Lagoon.

Preliminary plans for the African pavilion, for example, call for a tree-house overlooking a jungle watering hole. The simulated setting will include a diorama of trees with jungle sounds and scents blending over a rear-projection film of African animals.

In the meantime, some of the existing national pavilions will open new facilities. Besides Germany and Japan, the United Kingdom and Italy have new shows or rides planned.

EPCOT Center Ride Information

— Cutting Down Your Time in Line by Understanding the Rides —

EPCOT Center has fewer rides overall than the Magic Kingdom (see "Cutting Down Your Time in Line by Understanding the Rides," Magic Kingdom, page 66). All of them are major features of the park and rank on a par with Pirates of the Caribbean and the Jungle Cruise in the Magic Kingdom in terms of scope, detail, imagination, and spectacle. All but one or two EPCOT Center rides are fast loading with large overall carrying capacities. Thus, EPCOT Center rides are, on average, well engineered and very efficient. Lines at EPCOT Center are often somewhat longer than in the Magic Kingdom, but usually move quickly. There are no amusement park rides at EPCOT Center and no rides which are specifically intended for children. All of the rides currently operating at EPCOT Center are located in Future World except for El Rio del Tiempo boat ride in the Mexican pavilion.

In the Magic Kingdom traffic flow is to some extent a function of the popularity and engineering of individual rides. At EPCOT Center traffic flow is much more affected by the way the park is laid out. In terms of touring efficiency it is important to understand how the Magic Kingdom rides operate. At EPCOT Center this knowledge is decidedly less important.

While technical knowledge of the rides at EPCOT Center is not necessarily essential to efficient touring, some background will assist you in estimating how long you may have to wait in line for a particular ride. "Duration of Ride" refers to the time you are actually riding. "Loading Method" refers to how the ride loads and unloads passengers; this is detailed in the section on understanding rides in the Magic Kingdom, page 66. "Loading Speed" is a comparative description of how quickly the ride loads. "System Capacity" refers to the approximate number of passengers the ride will carry in an hour.

—— *Future World* ——

Spaceship Earth

See in the first half hour the park is open. Lines are somewhat shorter between 5 P.M. and 7 P.M. on many days.

Duration of Ride: Approximately 16 minutes

Average Wait in Line per 100 People: 3 minutes

Assumes: 140 or more cars operating

Loading Method: Continuous

Loading Speed: Moderate to fast

System Capacity: Approximately 2,000 persons per hour

Universe of Energy

See before 10:30 A.M. or in the late afternoon and evening.

NOTE: While there is a ride component to this attraction, it loads and unloads en masse in the manner of a theater. For technical information on the Universe of Energy, see the EPCOT Center Theater Information, page 137.

Horizons

See before 10:30 A.M. or after 3:30 P.M.

Duration of Ride: Approximately 15 minutes

Average Wait in Line per 100 People: 4 minutes

Assumes: Normal operation

Loading Method: Continuous

Loading Speed: Moderate to fast

System Capacity: 1,750 persons per hour

The Living Seas

See before 10 A.M. or after 5 P.M.

NOTE: The Living Seas is a combination ride and theater experience.

Duration of Presentation: 6-minute movie followed by a 3-minute ride

The Living Seas (continued)

Average Wait in Line per 100 People: 3½ minutes
Loading Method: Continuous
Loading Speed: Moderate to fast
System Capacity: 2,000 persons per hour

World of Motion

It's Fun to Be Free

See any time of day (lines are longest just following exodus of audience from nearby Universe of Energy).

Duration of Ride: Approximately 14½ minutes
Average Wait in Line per 100 People: 2¾ minutes
Assumes: Normal operation
Loading Method: Continuous
Loading Speed: Moderate to fast
System Capacity: Approximately 2,200 persons per hour

Journey into Imagination

Journey into Imagination Ride

See before 11:30 A.M. or after 5:30 P.M.

Duration of Ride: Approximately 13 minutes
Average Wait in Line per 100 People: 3 minutes
Assumes: 20 trains operating
Loading Method: Continuous
Loading Speed: Moderate to fast
System Capacity: Approximately 1,750 persons per hour

The Land

Listen to the Land

See before 11 A.M. or after 4 P.M.

Duration of Ride: Approximately 12 minutes
Average Wait in Line per 100 People: 3 minutes
Assumes: 15 boats operating
Loading Method: Interval

Loading Speed: Moderate to fast

System Capacity: Approximately 2,100 persons per hour

— *World Showcase* —

Mexico

El Rio del Tiempo

See before 11 A.M. or after 6:30 P.M.

Duration of Ride: Approximately 7 minutes (plus 1½-minute wait to disembark)

Average Wait in Line per 100 People: 4½ minutes

Assumes: 16 boats in operation

Loading Method: Interval

Loading Speed: Moderate

System Capacity: Approximately 1,300 persons per hour

EPCOT Center
Theater Information

— *Cutting Down Your Time in Line*
by Understanding the Shows —

By a show we are referring to a theater performance as opposed to a ride. EPCOT Center, unlike the Magic Kingdom, offers more theater presentations than rides. While not as complex from a crowd management perspective as many of the rides, a little enlightenment concerning the operation of the various theater attractions may save some valuable touring time.

Theater attractions at EPCOT Center operate in three distinct phases:

1. There is the audience who is actually in the theater viewing the presentation.

2. There are the visitors who have passed through the turnstile into a holding area or waiting lobby. These people will be admitted to the theater as soon as the presentation currently in progress is concluded.

3. There is the outside line. Those waiting here will be admitted to the waiting lobby when there is room, and will ultimately move from the waiting lobby to the theater.

Most of the theaters at EPCOT Center hold a lot of people. Thus when a new audience is admitted to the theater the outside line (if there is one) will usually disappear. Except on extremely busy days the maximum wait for a given theater presentation should be no longer than twice the time of the performance itself.

Theater capacity and the popularity of the presentation, along with the level of attendance in the park determines how long you will have to wait in line to see a particular show. The following gives specific information concerning each theater attraction that should help you plan your visit. See pages 117–31 for descriptions of the respective presentations.

136

—— *Future World* ——

Universe of Energy

Type: Mixed media and Audio-Animatronics presentation about energy

When to Go: Before 10:30 A.M. and after 4:30 P.M.

Duration of Presentation: Approximately 26½ minutes

Preshow Entertainment: 8 minutes

Theater Capacity per Performance: 2 theaters each with a capacity of 580 persons

Theater Capacity: Approximately 2,200 persons per hour

CommuniCore East

Backstage Magic

Type: A look at the EPCOT Center computer control room

When to Go: After 6 P.M.

Duration of Presentation: Approximately 17 minutes

Preshow Entertainment: None

Theater Capacity per Performance: Approximately 130 persons

Theater Capacity: Approximately 400 persons per hour

The Land

Kitchen Kabaret

Type: Audio-Animatronics kitchen variety show

When to Go: Before 11 A.M. and after 2:30 P.M.

Duration of Presentation: Approximately 13 minutes

Preshow Entertainment: None

Theater Capacity per Performance: Approximately 250 persons

Theater Capacity: Approximately 1,000 persons per hour

Harvest Theater: Symbiosis

Type: Film exploring the relationship of man with his environment

When to Go: Before 11:30 A.M. and after 3 P.M.

Duration of Presentation: Approximately 18½ minutes

Harvest Theater: Symbiosis (continued)

Preshow Entertainment: None

Theater Capacity per Performance: Approximately 460 persons

Theater Capacity: Approximately 1,300 persons per hour

Journey into Imagination

*Magic Eye Theater: Magic Journeys**

Type: 3-D fantasy film

When to Go: Before 11:30 A.M. and after 5:30 P.M.

Duration of Presentation: Approximately 17 minutes

Preshow Entertainment: 8 minutes

Theater Capacity per Performance: Approximately 600 persons

Theater Capacity: Approximately 2,000 persons per hour

— *World Showcase* —

Canada

O Canada!

Type: Travel film

When to Go: Before 11 A.M. and after 3:30 P.M.

Duration of Presentation: Approximately 18 minutes

Preshow Entertainment: None

Theater Capacity per Performance: Approximately 570 persons

Theater Capacity: Approximately 2,000 persons per hour

France

Impressions de France

Type: Travel film

When to Go: Before 11 A.M. and after 7 P.M.

Duration of Presentation: Approximately 18 minutes

Preshow Entertainment: None

Theater Capacity per Performance: Approximately 350 persons

Theater Capacity: Approximately 950 persons per hour

*The film *Magic Journeys* is scheduled to be replaced sometime during 1986 by a Michael Jackson 3-D rock film.

United States

The American Adventure

Type: Mixed media and Audio-Animatronics presentation on U.S. history

When to Go: Before noon and after 2:30 P.M.

Duration of Presentation: Approximately 29 minutes

Preshow Entertainment: None

Theater Capacity per Performance: Approximately 1,000 persons

Theater Capacity: Approximately 2,000 persons per hour

China

Wonders of China

Type: Travel film

When to Go: Anytime

Duration of Presentation: Approximately 19 minutes

Preshow Entertainment: None

Theater Capacity per Performance: Approximately 1,000 persons

Theater Capacity: Approximately 2,600 persons per hour

Live Entertainment in EPCOT Center

Live entertainment in EPCOT Center is somewhat more diversified, as might be expected, than that of the Magic Kingdom. World Showcase provides almost unlimited potential for representative entertainment from the respective nations, and Future World allows for a new wave of creativity in live entertainment offerings.

Some information concerning the live entertainment on the day of your visit can be obtained from the information desk in the Earth Station lobby. Our experience, however, indicates that the Earth Station attendants are not usually too well informed. Another source of information is the WorldKey Information Service. WorldKey usually has the answers, but it is not as direct as quizzing an attendant. EPCOT Center, like the Magic Kingdom, is very lax and inconsistent about having any sort of printed handout available concerning the day's performances.

Listed below are some of the performers and performances you are likely to encounter. In addition, fireworks over the World Showcase Lagoon and a daily parade are being planned.

Future World Brass	A roving brass band that marches and plays according to a more or less extemporaneous schedule near Spaceship Earth and at other Future World locations.
Robot Characters	Costumed characters who lurk in the CommuniCore area of Future World, playing with children and posing for pictures.
American Gardens Stage	The site of EPCOT Center's premier live performances is near The American Adventure, facing World Showcase Lagoon, in a large amphitheater. Top talent imported from all over the world play the American Gardens

Stage on a limited engagement basis. Many shows highlight the music, dance, and costume of the performers' home country.

LaserPhonic Fantasy

An after dark show, consisting of music, fireworks, erupting fountains, special lighting, and laser technology performed on the World Showcase lagoon when the park is open late.

Around World Showcase

A variety of unscheduled, impromptu performances take place in and around the various pavilions of World Showcase. You may encounter a strolling mariachi group in Mexico, street actors in Italy, a fife and drum corps or a singing group (The Voices of Liberty) at The American Adventure, traditional songs and dances in Japan, comical street musicians (the Pearly Kings and Queens) and a bagpipe band in England, white-faced mimes in France, and a versatile musical group, the Maple Leaf Brass, in Canada.

Dinner Shows

The restaurants in World Showcase as well as the Odyssey Restaurant, serve up healthy portions of live entertainment to accompany the victuals. Examples of restaurant floorshow fare include folk dancers and a baskapelle band in Germany, singing waiters in Italy, and electronic music at the Odyssey. Restaurant shows are performed at both lunch and dinner seatings. Reservations are required (see "Eating in EPCOT Center," below) except at the Odyssey.

Eating in EPCOT Center

One of EPCOT Center's big claims is that "it will always be in a state of becoming"—that is, it will always be expanding and updating its facilities and attractions. It is to be devoutly hoped that EPCOT Center is in "a state of becoming" better at food service.

There is this to say: The quality and variety of food at EPCOT Center is considerably better than that available in the Magic Kingdom or in the Theme Resort Hotels, probably because there is such an emphasis on sit-down restaurants as opposed to fast-food places. But for all their expertise at crowd handling, the Disney people are no better at dealing with all the hungry visitors at EPCOT Center than they are in the Magic Kingdom.

Making arrangements for meals can literally consume hours of your time; first standing in line to make reservations (twice if you want a sit-down meal at both lunch and dinner), then later abandoning or re-arranging your touring plan to scurry to the designated restaurant at the appointed seating time, and finally waiting for your table to be vacated, cleared, and readied for your use. Eating is such a hassle in EPCOT Center that ordinarily we would recommend just snacking and avoiding major meals entirely. However, the restaurants are such an integral part of World Showcase in particular that we think it would be a mistake not to have a meal in at least one of them.

—— Getting a Handle on the World Showcase Restaurants ——

Obtaining a reservation for a particular restaurant is a function of its popularity and seating capacity, and, of course, the size of the crowd on the day of your visit. Each restaurant has seatings for both lunch and dinner. Reservations must be made on the day of the meal.

To insure the restaurant and seating of your choice, arrive at the entrance turnstiles, passport in hand, 45 minutes before EPCOT Center opens. Upon admission proceed posthaste to Earth Station (the building at the base of the dome). Both lunch and dinner reservations can be made at the same time. Be prepared with alternatives for both restaurants and seatings in case your first choices are filled. If there are several folks in your party, perhaps one might volunteer to make the restaurant reservations while the others ride Spaceship Earth. Spaceship Earth disembarks passengers into Earth Station thus making it fairly easy to regroup.

Failure to follow the foregoing directions will result in a forty-five-minute-or-longer wait in line to make reservations with no guarantee that anything will be available. On most days the World Showcase restaurants book solid for preferred seating times within an hour to an hour and a half of the park opening. Even if you get a reservation, you will have expended your most productive/crowd-free touring time in the process.

If you blow it and arrive late but still want to eat in one of the World Showcase restaurants, here are some strategies that often pay off:

1. Go to a WorldKey Information terminal *outside* of Earth Station (there are some located around the bridgeway connecting Future World to World Showcase) and use the system as described on page 115 to call up an attendant. Try to make a reservation.

2. If you can't get a reservation via WorldKey, go to the restaurant of your choice and apply at the door for a reservation. Sometimes only lunch reservations are taken at the door, but lunch and dinner menus are comparable if not the same. Just have your main meal at lunch.

3. If neither of the foregoing work, go to the restaurant of your choice and ask the hostess to call you if she gets a cancellation. A reservation is held about 15–20 minutes before the vacancy is filled with "standby" diners. Very early and very late seatings have a greater incidence of no-shows.

4. If the options mentioned above do not pan out, try Le Cellier, a cafeteria in the Canadian pavilion, or have a member of your group try for a dinner reservation at the door of the Good Turn Restaurant (upper floor of the Land pavilion) as you pass through the Land on your tour.

— The Restaurants of EPCOT Center —

While eating at EPCOT Center can be a consumate hassle, it is likewise true that an afternoon in the World Showcase section of EPCOT Center without a dinner reservation is something like not having a date on the day of the prom. Each pavilion has its beautifully seductive ethnic eatery offering the hungry tourist the gastronomic delights of the world. To tour one after another of these exotic foreign settings and not partake is almost beyond the limits of willpower.

In all honesty, the food in some of the World Showcase restaurants is not very compelling, but the overall experience is exhilarating. And if you fail to avail yourself of a meal in the World Showcase, you will correctly deduce that you have missed out on one of EPCOT Center's more delightful features.

In our opinion there is no logical correlation between price, quality, and popularity of the World Showcase restaurants. Our researchers, for example, found L'Originale Alfredo di Roma Ristorante (Italy) frequently disappointing in spite of the fact that it is almost always one of the first two restaurants to fill its seatings. To assist you in making your choice, a data summary of each World Showcase restaurant requiring reservations (plus the Canadian Le Cellier) is presented below.

Canada

Le Cellier (No Reservations Required)

This is the only cafeteria-style restaurant in the World Showcase and represents a tasty and economical choice for those who want a nicer meal but do not have reservations elsewhere.

Time to go: Lunch—before 11:30 and after 2:00
Dinner—before 5:30 and after 8:00

United Kingdom

Rose & Crown Pub & Dining Room (Reservations Required)

Seating Capacity: 152

Popularity: More popular for lunch. About the fifth to book for dinner, owing more to its small size than to its popularity.

Critic's Rating: Hearty but nothing to get excited about.

Atmosphere: Excellent, warm pub interior with an unparalleled view of the World Showcase Lagoon.

Price: Moderate.

Entertainment: Madrigal music with lute.

Comments: Fish & chips, steak and kidney pie, roast beef and basic pub fare make up the menu here.

France

Les Chefs de France (Reservations Required)

Seating Capacity: 162

Popularity: Usually the second restaurant to fill its reservations.

Critic's Rating: Very good and sometimes excellent.

Atmosphere: Elegant and bright, but not intimate or romantic.

Price: Expensive.

Entertainment: None.

Comments: Les Chefs apply their art with great success to fresh Florida seafood.

Le Bistro de Paris (Reservations Required)

Seating Capacity: 150

Popularity: Very popular. Many patrons make reservations here by mistake, thinking they are scheduling for Les Chefs.

Critic's Rating: Good, but lacking the creativity and delicacy of Les Chefs.

Atmosphere: Bright and bustling.

Price: Moderate to Expensive.

Entertainment: None.

Comments: A good choice for picky American "meat and potato" diners. Specializes in continental peasant fare.

Morocco

El Marrakech (Reservations Required)

Seating Capacity: 250

Popularity: Normally the sixth or seventh restaurant to fill its reservations.

Critic's Rating: Different, usually good; portions sometimes skimpy.

Atmosphere: Colorful and exotic.

Price: Moderate.

El Marrakech (*continued*)

Entertainment: Belly dancing and a Moroccan band.

Comments: Interesting fare almost impossible to find except in the largest of U.S. cities.

Japan

Mitsukoshi Restaurant (Reservations Required)

Seating Capacity: Teppanyaki Dining, 160; Tempura Kiku, 27

Popularity: Normally the third or fourth restaurant to fill its reservations.

Critic's Rating: Nothing to write home about. Eschews the diverse and beautiful traditional Japanese fare for teppan table cooking a la the Benihana of Tokyo chain restaurants. Sushi and sashimi are not currently available.

Atmosphere: Enchanting stained wood and paper wall traditional Japanese surroundings.

Price: Moderate to Expensive.

Entertainment: Provided by the chopping, juggling teppan chefs.

Comments: This restaurant has missed a wonderful opportunity to introduce authentic Japanese cuisine to the American public. The menu in this eatery is nothing less than a cop-out, i.e., don't expect a meaningful introduction to Japanese food at Mitsukoshi. If you go, we recommend the Tempura Kiku, a small section of the dining room specializing in tempura. Finally, be aware that diners at the teppan tables (large tables with a flattop grill in the middle) are seated at a common table with other parties.

Italy

L'Originale Alfredo di Roma Ristorante (Reservations Required)

Seating Capacity: 254

Popularity: Usually the first restaurant to fill its seating.

Critic's Rating: Overrated and somewhat overpriced. Our guess is that many diners feel more familiar with Italian food than with the other ethnic cuisines available at EPCOT Center, thus making Alfredo's popular beyond its ability to deliver.

Atmosphere: Elegant, bright, with beautiful murals adorning several walls.

Price: Moderate, but overpriced for pasta entrées.

Entertainment: Wonderfully talented singing waiters and waitresses erupting in a profusion of song, including Italian traditional, classical, and opera.

Comments: If you go try veal or chicken. If you must have pasta, order an appetizer portion or a side dish.

China

Nine Dragons (Reservations Required)

Seating Capacity: 200

Popularity: Usually the third or fourth restaurant to fill its reservations.

Atmosphere: Traditional Chinese.

Price: Moderate.

Comments: A much-needed addition to the World Showcase.

Germany

Biergarten (Reservations Required)

Seating Capacity: 360

Popularity: Usually the fifth or sixth to book its reservations.

Critic's Rating: Food is hearty. The dinner show is fun and rousing, and the overall atmosphere is festive.

Atmosphere: The largest of the reservation restaurants. Multiple tiers of diners surround a stage where yodelers, dancers, and a German band perform in the evening at each scheduled seating. The beer flows freely and diners join in the singing, making the Biergarten a happy, delightful place to dine.

Price: Moderate.

Entertainment: Yodelers, dancers, singers, and a German band.

Comments: Some of the German specialties on the menu have been modified a la the Disney tradition of conforming to the tastes of the average. Best bets are the "wursts and the spitted chicken." Because of the size of the Biergarten, it is an above average bet for getting in without a reservation as a "standby."

Mexico

San Angel Inn Restaurante (Reservations Required)

Seating Capacity: 158

Popularity: Usually the third or fourth restaurant to fill its reservations.

Critic's Rating: Excellent food and excellent value.

Atmosphere: Superb, truly romantic. You sit beneath the stars in a re-creation of a small village on the banks of the Rio del Tiempo with the jungle and an Aztec pyramid in the background.

Price: Moderate.

Entertainment: None.

Comments: Delightful menu goes beyond the normal Mexican fare, offering regional and special dishes that are very difficult to find in the U.S. Our choice for the best all-around restaurant in EPCOT Center.

Future World Reservation Restaurants

Future World restaurants are primarily fast-food establishments. There are, however, two exceptions, and both are worthy competitors in terms of food quality, atmosphere, and menu creativity of the World Showcase ethnic restaurants. What's more, they are sometimes forgotten in the great morning reservations rush.

The Land Pavilion

Good Turn Restaurant (Reservations Required)

Seating Capacity: 232

Popularity: Most popular at lunch. Often overlooked for dinner.

Critic's Rating: Good food and creative menu. A good choice for finicky eaters and beef-and-potato lovers.

Atmosphere: Elegant revolving platform which overlooks rain forest, prairie, and farm scenes along the Listen to the Land boat-ride route. Unexpectedly intimate and romantic.

Price: Moderate plus.

Entertainment: None.

Comments: A nice change of pace. The only full-service restaurant in EPCOT Center that serves breakfast.

Living Seas Pavilion

Coral Reef Restaurant (Reservations Required)

Seating Capacity: 250

Popularity: Popular because of its novelty and fresh seafood specialty.

Critic's Rating: Walt Disney World chefs have been making a name for themselves in seafood cooking competitions. The Coral Reef should prove to be a showcase for their best work.

Atmosphere: Diners eat fresh seafood and are surrounded by even fresher (live) seafood. Very interesting.

Price: Moderate plus.

Comments: Open January 1986.

Alternatives and Suggestions for Eating in EPCOT Center

Listed below are some suggestions for any dauntless, epicurean adventurer who is determined to eat at EPCOT Center:

1. Do not stand in lines at restaurants unless absolutely necessary. Use the WorldKey terminals (calling up an attendant) to make your reservations.

2. For fast-food meals, EPCOT Center is like the Magic Kingdom (except there is not enough supply to meet the demand); eat before 11 A.M. or after 2 P.M. The Odyssey Restaurant and the Liberty Inn at the United States pavilion move people through pretty speedily, and sometimes you can get served in a reasonable time in The Land pavilion (the latter being a bit more iffy). Some of the food at The Land is a cut above the average; as for the other fast-food places mentioned, expect bulk.

3. Review the "Alternatives and Suggestions for Eating in the Magic Kingdom," page 84. Many tips for the Magic Kingdom also apply to EPCOT Center.

Shopping in EPCOT Center

The shops in Future World seem a little out of place, the atmosphere being too visionary and grandiose to accommodate the pettiness of the bargain table. Similarly, it obviously has been difficult to find merchandise consistent with the surroundings. Expressed differently, what is available for purchase in Future World is also available at a lot of other places (EPCOT and Disney trademark souvenirs being the exception).

The World Showcase shops add a lot of realism and atmosphere to the street scenes of which they are part. But it's the same high-priced merchandise which, for the most part, could be found on the shelves of better boutiques, import shops, and department stores almost anywhere in the nation.

EPCOT Center
One-Day Touring Plans

The EPCOT Center One-Day Touring Plans are field-tested, step-by-step itineraries for seeing all of the major attractions at EPCOT Center in one day with a minimum of waiting in line. They are designed to keep you ahead of the crowds while the park is filling in the morning and to place you at the less crowded attractions during EPCOT Center's busier hours of the day. They assume that you would be happier doing a *little* extra walking as opposed to a lot of extra standing in line.

Touring EPCOT Center in one day is much more strenuous and demanding than touring the Magic Kingdom in a single day. To begin with, EPCOT Center is about twice the physical size of the Magic Kingdom. Secondly, and unlike the Magic Kingdom, EPCOT Center has essentially no effective in-park transportation system; wherever you want to go, it's always quicker and easier to walk. Where visitors arriving at the Magic Kingdom disperse rather evenly, visitors arriving at EPCOT Center tend to cluster. Spaceship Earth forms immense lines ten minutes after opening while the rest of the park is virtually empty. The One-Day Touring Plans will assist you in avoiding crowds and bottlenecks on days of moderate to heavy attendance, but cannot lessen the distance you will have to walk. Wear comfortable shoes and be prepared for a lot of hiking. On days of lighter attendance, when crowd conditions are not a critical factor, the Touring Plans will serve primarily to help you organize your tour.

On days of moderate to heavy attendance follow the Touring Plans exactly; do not deviate from them except:

1. When you do not want to experience an attraction called for on the Touring Plans—if an attraction is listed that does not interest you, simply skip that step and proceed to the next step.

2. When you encounter an extremely long line at an attraction called for by the Touring Plans—the central idea is to avoid crowds, not to join them. Crowds build and dissipate throughout the day for a variety

of reasons. The Touring Plans anticipate most normally recurring crowd-flow patterns but cannot predict spontaneously arising situations (Spaceship Earth breaking down, for instance, with the hundreds of people standing in line suddenly descending on the nearby Universe of Energy). If the line is ridiculously long, simply skip that step and move on to the next, coming back later for another try.

Two outline versions of One-Day Touring Plans follow this section; each is tailored for groups with different needs.

—— *Traffic Patterns in EPCOT Center* ——

After admiring for many years the way traffic is engineered at the Magic Kingdom, we were somewhat amazed at the way EPCOT Center was laid out. At the Magic Kingdom, Main Street, U.S.A., with its many shops and eateries, serves as a huge gathering place when the park opens and subsequently funnels visitors to the central hub from which branch entrances, each equally accessible, to the various lands. Thus are the crowds first welcomed and entertained (on Main Street) and then distributed almost equally to the respective lands. At EPCOT Center, by contrast, Spaceship Earth, the park's premier architectural landmark and one of its featured attractions, is situated just inside the main entrance. When visitors enter the park they invariably and almost irresistibly head right for it. Hence crowds tend to bottleneck as soon as the park opens less than seventy-five yards from the admission turnstiles. For those in the know, however, the congestion at Spaceship Earth provides some excellent opportunities for escaping waits at other rides and shows in the Future World section of EPCOT Center. If you are one of the first in the gate do not hesitate to experience Spaceship Earth (you will probably not find a shorter line later). If Spaceship Earth lines wind around the side of adjoining Earth Station, pass by the ride.

Early morning crowds are contained in the Future World half of EPCOT Center for the simple reason that the World Showcase half does not open until later in the morning. Distribution of visitors to the various Future World attractions, except Spaceship Earth, is fairly equal. Many of the early visitors to CommuniCore West and the attractions located behind it arrive by accident while trying to find the end of the line to Spaceship Earth. Morning visitors trying to move counter to the main traffic flow would bypass Spaceship Earth (unless the line was short) and proceed directly to The Land, and from there to Journey into Imagination.

When World Showcase, the other main section of EPCOT Center, opens (usually at 10 A.M.), most early visitors are still touring Future World. Thus the opening of World Showcase does not have a dramatic effect on the distribution of visitors to the overall park. Or expressed differently, between 10 A.M. and 11 A.M. there are more people entering Future World via the entrance than departing Future World into World Showcase. Attendance continues building in Future World until sometime between noon and 2 P.M. World Showcase attendance builds rapidly with the approach of the midday meal. Exhibits at the far end of World Showcase Lagoon report playing to full capacity audiences from about noon on through 6:30 P.M.–7:30 P.M.

The central focus of World Showcase in the eyes of most visitors is its atmosphere featuring international landmarks, romantic street scenes, quaint shops, and ethnic restaurants. Unlike the Magic Kingdom with its premier rides and attractions situated along the far perimeters of its respective lands, World Showcase has only one major entertainment draw, *The American Adventure.* Thus, where the Magic Kingdom uses its super attractions to draw and distribute the crowds rather evenly, there is only one such draw in World Showcase (compared to six or seven in Future World). With the exception of making restaurant reservations, therefore, there is no compelling reason to rush to the World Showcase section of the park. The bottom line in Future World is a preponderance of people which builds all morning and into the early afternoon. The two main sections of EPCOT Center do not approach equality in attendance until the approach of the evening meal. It should be stated, however, that evening crowds in World Showcase do not compare with the size of morning and midday crowds in Future World. Attendance throughout EPCOT Center is normally lighter in the evening.

An interesting observation at EPCOT Center from a crowd-distribution perspective is the indifference of repeat visitors relative to favoring one attraction over another. At the Magic Kingdom repeat visitors make a mad dash for their favorite ride and their preferences are strong and well defined. At EPCOT Center, by contrast, many returning tourists indicate that (with the possible exceptions of Spaceship Earth and *The American Adventure*) they enjoy the major rides and features "about the same." The conclusion suggested here is that touring patterns at EPCOT Center will be more systematic and predictable (i.e., by the numbers, clockwise, counterclockwise, etc.) than at the Magic Kingdom.

Closing time at EPCOT Center does not precipitate congestion similar to that observed when the Magic Kingdom closes. One primary reason for the ease of departure from EPCOT Center is that its parking lot is adjacent to the park as opposed to being separated by a lake as in the Magic Kingdom. At the Magic Kingdom, departing visitors bottleneck at the monorail to the Transportation and Ticket Center and main parking lot. At EPCOT Center you can proceed directly to your car. A second reason for diminished closing time crowds is the practice of usually closing the Future World section of the park an hour or so before World Showcase closes.

EPCOT Center One-Day Touring Plan for Adults

FOR: **Adults without small children.**

ASSUMES: Willingness to experience all major rides and shows.

DIRECTION	EXPLANATION
1. Have your admission paid and be at the turnstile ready to go forty-five minutes before the park's stated opening time. NOTE: EPCOT Center often opens a half hour before its stated opening time.	Being one of the first visitors admitted to the park will allow you to see many of the most popular attractions at the time of day when the lines are shortest. The thirty to forty-five minutes you invest in your early morning arrival will literally save you hours during the remainder of your touring day.
2. When you are admitted to the park proceed posthaste to Spaceship Earth (the huge geodesic dome just inside the entrance). If your top priority is obtaining reservations for a World Showcase lunch or dinner, skip Spaceship Earth until late afternoon and proceed directly to Step 3. If you want to have your cake and eat it too, find someone in your party who will volunteer to forego Spaceship Earth and have him run ahead to make meal reservations while you take the ride. He can meet you inside Earth Station where the ride disembarks.	Spaceship Earth, because of its theme, distinctive design, and positioning near the entrance to the park, develops an incredible line mere minutes after EPCOT Center opens. Moreover, because of the attraction's popularity, the line remains quite long all day. The only shot you have, therefore, of avoiding a 45-minute or longer wait for Spaceship Earth is to hop in line during the first few minutes that the park is open. A short line for Spaceship Earth (30-minute wait) is one which fills the attraction's queue area (the system of parallel railings situated in front of Spaceship Earth). A medium line would completely fill the queue area and would additionally extend down the sidewalk to the right (west side) of Earth Station.

DIRECTION	EXPLANATION

A medium line usually corresponds to a wait of 35 to 55 minutes. A long line for Spaceship Earth extends past Earth Station and into the open area between CommuniCore East and West. Waiting time for a long line is from one to three hours. If the line you encounter is short to mid-medium, go ahead and see Spaceship Earth. *If the line is longer, bypass Spaceship Earth for the time being.*

3. Go directly to a WorldKey Information video display terminal and make restaurant reservations for lunch and dinner. We recommend asking for a late seating for dinner (8 P.M.–9 P.M.). This will allow maximum touring flexibility in the itinerary and take advantage of the fact that World Showcase usually stays open later than Future World. If your tummy throws a fit, grab a snack around 5 P.M. to tide you over.

The better restaurants at EPCOT Center are sit-down restaurants requiring reservations which must be made on the same day that you plan to dine. Some visitors walk to the eatery of their choice and stand in line for reservations. By far an easier approach is to make reservations when you first arrive via the WorldKey Information Service. There are many WorldKey terminals scattered around the park, but the largest number are situated on the far side of Earth Station opposite where you exit the Spaceship Earth ride. For greater elaboration see "Eating in EPCOT Center," page 142, and the special section on the WorldKey Information Service, page 115. If you only have one day to visit the EPCOT Center, you may be better off making a reservation for dinner only and having a fast-food lunch.

DIRECTION	EXPLANATION
4. Go directly to The Living Seas and enjoy the tour (open January 1986).	This is a new and popular ride, and the best time to catch it is in the morning.
5. Go directly to The Land, situated behind CommuniCore West and take the boat trip, Listen to the Land.	The Land pavilion consists of three attractions and a variety of restaurants. The best way to see this attraction is to arrive early before the restaurant crowd hits. On a One-Day Touring Plan we bypass for the time being the other two attractions here.
6. Proceed to Journey into Imagination, the next big pavilion to the right of The Land. Ride Journey into Imagination first, then see the 3-D film, *Magic Journeys*, at the Magic Eye Theater.	Following this Touring Plan, you should arrive at Journey into Imagination before attendance gets particularly heavy. Ride first and then see the movie for most efficient crowd avoidance.
7. Exit Future World and proceed directly to World Showcase.	By this time crowds will be building throughout the Future World section of the park. Leave Future World and proceed to World Showcase where crowds will not as yet have reached their peak.
8. Bypassing Canada and England for the time being, go directly to France and see the film *Impressions de France*.	By moving directly to the far end of World Showcase Lagoon you can reach the French and American exhibits before they become extremely crowded. The French exhibit, particularly, becomes quite congested as the noon hour approaches.
9. Go directly to the American pavilion and see *The American*	This is a large-capacity theater production which will accommo-

DIRECTION	EXPLANATION
Adventure.	date large numbers of viewers even when the park is busy.
10. If the lines are not prohibitive (and if you did not make reservations for a sit-down lunch) grab a bite to eat at the Liberty Inn, or quicker yet, at the bratwurst stand on the left side of Germany.	With the exception of some street vendors, this is the only source of fast-food meals in the immediate area. Liberty Inn is quite large and can probably serve more food to more people in less time than any other restaurant in World Showcase. If you are not hungry, stop later for a bratwurst from the street vendor in Germany.
11. Whether you eat or not, go next to the Japanese exhibit and from there proceed in a counter-clockwise direction to Italy, Germany, and the People's Republic of China. At the Chinese exhibit see the film *Wonders of China.*	The entire park will be very busy by this time of day. Enjoy the atmosphere of the respective international pavilions.
12. Bypass Mexico for the time being and reenter Future World; see the World of Motion.	This is a continuous loading ride where the wait in line is almost always tolerable.
13. Go next door and tour Horizons.	This is a continuously loading ride where the line is almost always tolerable except when the audience of a just-concluded Universe of Energy performance (next pavilion in the direction of the dome) descends en masse. If you encounter long lines at Horizons any time during the evening, just take a break; they will usually work themselves out in about 10–15 minutes.

DIRECTION	EXPLANATION
14. Next, go to the Universe of Energy and ask an attendant what the anticipated wait will be. If less than 45 minutes, stay and see the show, otherwise, proceed to Step 15.	Lines at the Universe of Energy vary considerably in length (owing in part to the unreliable nature of nearby Spaceship Earth, which breaks down frequently, dispersing its masses of waiting people primarily to Universe of Energy). If you catch Universe of Energy at a bad time, skip it for the present and try again later. If you can get in in less than 45 minutes, bite the bullet and hop in line.
15. Cross through CommuniCore and return to The Land. See the film *Symbiosis* at the Harvest Theater and a performance of the Kitchen Kabaret.	The lunch crowd will be gone by the time you return to The Land. See whichever of the two productions begins sooner, followed by the other. This is a good time and place to grab a snack if your dinner reservation is for a late seating as recommended.
16. While in Future World, see Spaceship Earth and/or Universe of Energy if you missed them earlier.	Spaceship Earth will have its shortest lines between 5:30 P.M. and 7:30 P.M. (which only means that the lines will be comparatively short; expect at least a forty-five minute wait). Lines at the Universe of Energy should be tolerable unless some other nearby attraction is not operating.
17. Backtrack to the World Showcase and see England followed by Canada; at Canada see the film *O Canada!*	Be sure to see England first and then Canada.
18. An hour or so before your dinner seating go to Mexico and ride El Rio del Tiempo, the River of Time.	This ride has long lines until after 6 P.M. on most days.

DIRECTION	EXPLANATION

19. Proceed to dinner.

20. After dinner, if you have any time or energy left, visit or revisit the EPCOT Center attractions of your choice.

NOTE: EPCOT Center One-Day Touring Plan for Adults operates under the assumption that you are willing to do some extra walking to avoid long waits in line. There is, therefore, some backtracking involved. Visitors adhering closely to the Touring Plan and moving expeditiously from Steps 1 through 9 particularly, will normally be able to see almost the entire park in a single day with an acceptable pace and minimal waits in line.

— *Outline of EPCOT Center One-Day Touring Plan, for Adults* —

1. Pay your admission and be waiting at the turnstiles forty-five minutes before the park's stated opening time. Remember, sometimes EPCOT Center opens a half hour before its stated opening time. Therefore, if the stated opening time is 9 A.M. be on site and ready to go at 8:15 A.M.

2. Go quickly and directly to Spaceship Earth—if the lines are short to mid-medium (see Step 2 in the elaborated version), go ahead and ride; if the lines exceed acceptable length, bypass until the evening hours. If restaurant reservations are a top priority, skip Spaceship Earth and go directly to Step 3.

3. Use the WorldKey Information terminals in the Earth Station lobby to make meal reservations. Try to get a late (8 P.M.–9 P.M.) seating.

4. Go directly to The Living Seas and enjoy the tour (open January 1986).

5. Proceed directly to The Land—take the boat trip Listen to the Land.

6. Go next to Journey into Imagination—ride Journey into Imagination; in the same pavilion view the 3-D movie at the Magic Eye Theater.

7. Go back through CommuniCore West (without stopping) and depart the Future World section of the park.

8. Bypass Canada and England for the moment; go directly to France and see *Impressions de France*.

9. Go past Japan for the time being to the American pavilion—see *The American Adventure*.

10. Eat lunch at the Liberty Inn if you are hungry and if the lines are not too long. If the lines are long try the bratwurst stand to the left of Germany.

11. Backtrack to tour the Japanese exhibit. From there proceed counterclockwise to tour Italy, Germany, and China; at China see the movie *Wonders of China*.

12. Bypass Mexico and reenter Future World—see the World of Motion.

13. Go to Horizons. If the line is long, take a 15-minute break and then return.

14. Go to the Universe of Energy—if the wait is less than forty-five minutes, stay for the show; otherwise proceed to Step 15.

15. Cross through CommuniCore and return to The Land—while there see the Kitchen Kabaret, and at the Harvest Theater, see *Symbiosis*. Grab a snack if you have reservations for a late dinner seating.

16. In Future World see Spaceship Earth and/or the Universe of Energy if you missed them earlier.

17. Backtrack to the World Showcase—go first to England and then to Canada; at Canada see *O Canada!*

18. An hour or so before your dinner seating go to Mexico and ride El Rio del Tiempo.

19. Proceed to dinner.

20. If the park is still open after dinner, visit or revisit the EPCOT Center attractions of your choice.

What You Missed

Nothing is missed on this EPCOT Center One-Day Touring Plan except for Backstage Magic in CommuniCore, and various live entertainments and special events which differ from day to day. Shops and stationary exhibits in both sections of the park, however, are accorded less priority on the Touring Plan than are films and rides, and some visitors may wish to substitute expanded time at the shops and exhibits for some of the other attractions.

— Outline of EPCOT Center One-Day Touring Plan, for Parents with Small Children —

FOR: **Adults with children under eight years of age.**

ASSUMES: Periodic stops for rest, restrooms, and refreshment.

EPCOT Center is educationally oriented and considerably more adult in tone and presentation than is the Magic Kingdom. Most younger children enjoy EPCOT Center if their visit is seven hours or less in duration, and if their tour emphasizes the Future World section of the park. Younger children, especially grade school children, find the international atmosphere of the World Showcase exciting, but do not have the patience for much more than a quick walk through. And while we found touring objectives of adults and younger children basically compatible in Future World, we noted that children tired quickly of the present World Showcase movies and shows (El Rio del Tiempo being an exception) and had a definite tendency to hurry their adult companions.

This EPCOT Center One-Day Touring Plan is designed to keep smaller children interested and happy without pushing them beyond the limits of their endurance. It is not a comprehensive touring plan, but attempts to balance a representative sampling of both sections of the park with the different interests and energy levels of children and adults.

1. Pay your admission and be waiting at the turnstiles forty-five minutes before the park opens. Remember, sometimes EPCOT Center opens a half hour before its stated opening time. If the stated opening time is 9 A.M., therefore, be on site and ready to go at 8:15 A.M.
2. Go quickly and directly to Spaceship Earth. If the lines are short to mid-medium (see Step 2 in the elaborated version), go ahead and ride; if the lines exceed acceptable length, bypass until later.
3. Stop at the Guest Relations desk in Earth Station (at the rear of Spaceship Earth) and obtain a schedule of live entertainment and special events for the day. Many of these offerings are particularly appealing to children and can be worked into the Touring Plan at your discretion.

4. Go directly to The Living Seas and enjoy the tour (open January 1986).

5. Proceed directly to The Land—take the boat trip Listen to the Land.

6. Go next to Journey into Imagination—ride Journey into Imagination; in the same pavilion view the 3-D movie at the Magic Eye Theater and visit the Image Works.

7. Go back through CommuniCore West (without stopping) and depart the Future World section of the park.

8. Go to Mexico—ride El Rio del Tiempo.

9. Proceed around the World Showcase Lagoon en route to *The American Adventure*, taking abbreviated tours of China, Germany, and Italy along the way. See *The American Adventure*.

10. Eat lunch at the Liberty Inn if you are hungry and if the lines are not too long. If the lines are long, obtain a snack from a sidewalk vendor and postpone lunch until you return to Future World.

11. Continue around World Showcase Lagoon stopping for quick visits at Japan, France, England, and Canada. At Canada see *O Canada!*

12. Reenter Future World—see the World of Motion.

13. Go to Horizons. If the line is long, take a 15-minute break and then return.

14. Go to the Universe of Energy—if the wait is less than forty-five minutes, stay for the show; otherwise proceed to Step 15.

15. Cross through CommuniCore and return to The Land—while there see the Kitchen Kabaret, and at the Harvest Theater, see *Symbiosis*. Grab something to eat if you missed lunch earlier.

16. If you missed Spaceship Earth and/or the Universe of Energy try them now.

17. Visit or revisit EPCOT Center attractions of your choice if you still have time and energy.

—— *Not to be Missed at EPCOT Center* ——

World Showcase	*The American Adventure*
Future World	Spaceship Earth
	Listen to the Land
	Journey into Imagination
	Magic Journeys
	It's Fun to Be Free
	Universe of Energy

EPCOT Center Summary
P.O. Box 40, Lake Buena Vista, FL 32380   Phone: (305) 824-4321
Call ahead for opening/closing times
Type: Futuristic and International Theme Park

Admission Costs

Ticket options	Adults	Children	Discounts	
One-Day Ticket	$18	$15	Children (3–17)	yes
3-Day World Passport	$45	$37	Children under 3	free
4-Day World Passport	$55	$45	Student	no
5-Day World Passport	$65	$53	Military	no
1-Year World Passport	$135	$110	Senior citizens	no
			Group rates	yes

Credit cards accepted for admission: **MasterCard and American Express**
Features included: **All**

*Overall Appeal**

By age groups	Preschool	Grade School[1]	Teens	Young Adults	Over 30	Senior Citizens
	***	***½	****	*****	*****	*****

Touring Tips

Touring time
  Average: **Full day**
  Minimum: Full day
Touring strategy: **See narrative**
Rainy day touring: **Recommended**

Periods of lightest attendance
  Time of day: **Early morning, late evening**
  Days: **Friday, Sunday**
  Times of year: **After Thanksgiving until 18th of December**

What the Critics Say

Rating of major features:
See pages 111–50

Rating of functional and operational areas

Parking	*****
Restrooms	*****
Resting places	*****
Crowd management	*****
Aesthetic appeal of grounds	*****
Cleanliness/maintenance	*****

Services and Facilities

Restaurant/snack bar **Yes**	Lockers **Yes**
Vending machines (food/pop) **No**	Pet kennels **Yes**
Alcoholic beverages **Yes**	Gift shops **Yes**
Handicapped access **Yes**	Film sales **Yes**
Wheelchairs **Rental**	Rain check **No**
Baby strollers **Rental**	Private guided group tours **Yes**

[1] Appreciation dependent on maturity of child

* Critical ratings are based on a scale of zero to five stars with five stars being the best possible rating.

Walt Disney World Index

See the following Magic Kingdom Attractions Index *and* EPCOT Center Attractions Index *for additional details.*

Magic Kingdom Attractions Index

EPCOT Center Attractions Index

— *About the Authors* —

Bob Sehlinger is a management consultant and author of five successful books on travel and recreation. John Finley is a twenty-year newspaper veteran, feature writer, and former travel and restaurant critic of the Pulitzer Prize–winning *Courier Journal* of Louisville, Kentucky.